MW01109158

CARRY ON!

Help and Hope for Life's Everyday Battles

David A. Skates

STANDARD
PUBLISHING
Cincinnati, Ohio

*To my wife,
whose words of love
and encouragement
helped me "carry on"
and complete this book.*

All Scripture quotations, unless otherwise indicated, are taken from the HOLY BIBLE, NEW INTERNATIONAL VERSION®. NIV®. Copyright © 1973, 1978, 1984 by International Bible Society. Used by permission of Zondervan Publishing House. All rights reserved.

SELECTED EXCERPT FROM PAGE 96 from PECULIAR TREASURES: A BIBLICAL WHO'S WHO by FREDERICK BUECHNER. Copyright © 1979 by Frederick Buechner. Reprinted by permission of HarperCollins Publishers, Inc.

Excerpts from THE FOUR LOVES by C. S. Lewis, copyright © 1960 by Helen Joy Lewis and renewed 1988 by Arthur Owen Barfield, reprinted by permission of Harcourt Brace & Company.

Library of Congress Cataloging-in-Publication Data

Skates, David
    Carry on! : help and hope for life's everyday battles / David Skates.
          p.   cm.
    Includes bibliographical references.
    ISBN 0-7847-0485-6
    1. Bible—Biography.   Virtues—Biblical teaching.   3. Virtues.
I. Title.
BS571.S538   1996
220.9'2—dc20   95-36271
                                                     CIP

Edited by Theresa C. Hayes
Cover design by Listenberger Design Associates

The Standard Publishing Company, Cincinnati, Ohio
A division of Standex International Corporation

03 02 01 00 99 98 97 96   5 4 3 2 1

Table of Contents

1   Introduction   5

2   The Meaning of Courage   9

3   Conquering Fear   21

4   Breaking the Grip of Guilt   31

5   Wrestling With Resentment   45

6   Dealing With Depression   57

7   Hope for Hostile Hearts   69

8   The Struggle for Self-Esteem   79

9   Building Lasting Friendships   89

10 The Perils of Peers   99

11 The Lure of Lust   111

12 When Temptation Knocks   123

13 Silver Threads Among the Gold   137

Introduction

William Faust turned off of Pacific Coast Highway and slowly headed up Topanga Canyon Boulevard. It was a crisp January evening in Southern California, one of those smogless winter days, chilly but not cold, a beautiful night for a drive. Cruising along the scenic canyon, Faust marveled at the beauty of the isolated area. He smiled as he thought about the millions of people living just minutes away. They seemed a thousand miles away.

Faust pulled over on the shoulder of the road. He wanted to breathe the clean air and stretch his legs. Walking off the road a few yards, he kicked a couple of rocks. A large piece of plywood lay on the ground. Faust playfully kicked it.

Before he knew what was happening, he was hurtling through space. With a sickening thud, he struck bottom. Slowly, he picked himself up; nothing seemed to be broken. Then his nose told him why. His thirty-foot fall had been cushioned by sewage and refuse. William Faust was at the bottom of a septic hole!

The stench was overpowering. Faust yelled until he was hoarse, but there was no reply. Slowly, he resigned himself to the fact that he would have to spend the night in the cesspool. In the morning, someone would notice his car and hear his voice. Until then, he resolved to make the best of it.

Faust's nose had almost adjusted to the stench when there was a small thud just inches away. A gopher had fallen into the septic hole! Bruised and afraid, the enraged gopher charged the startled twenty-five-year-old man.

And so William Faust spent that Sunday night in January fending off a crazed gopher while he stood up to his ankles in "deep do do." As one headline said, it was definitely "A night in deep trouble."[1]

Sometimes it seems that life is like that! People and problems come at us like ferocious gophers and the world smells like raw sewage.

This is a book about courage—the courage to face the "gophers" that attack us all. There is that fearsome duo of fear and guilt. There are the three gophers that charge us when we mishandle our anger: resentment, depression, and hostility. We all need to learn how better to handle their assaults in the strength of God and with the help only He can provide.

In addition, we all need courage to build solid, high quality, satisfying relationships. When our relationships are "right," life's great! When they aren't, we're back in the cesspool fighting gophers.

Finally, there's the cesspool of sensuality. Our society is awash in it, and only now are we beginning to admit that what was once called "free love" has a very high price tag, paid in the currency of broken homes, unwanted pregnancies, abortions, and sexually transmitted diseases. Even Christians are more strongly influenced by lust's leering line than most of us would care to admit. We will take time to look at some of God's eternal principles to help us to withstand temptations.

As I said, this book is essentially about courage—the courage to meet and conquer the problems, temptations, and difficult situations we all must face. As we discover how people of faith dealt with these issues in the past, may each of us find strength and hope for the future.

Join me on the journey!

"Courage is a man
who keeps on coming on.**"**

L. H. McNelly
Captain, Texas Rangers, 1844-77

"Courage is contagious.
When a brave man takes a stand,
the spines of others are stiffened.**"**

Billy Graham

"Be strong
and very courageous.
Be careful to obey all the law
my servant Moses gave you;
do not turn from it to the right
or to the left, that you may be
successful wherever you go.**"**

Joshua 1:7

Chapter One

The Meaning of Courage

It takes courage to confront fear, sin, and temptation. It takes courage to change. But what is "courage"? It is often misunderstood, yet it is something each of us is capable of achieving.

The year was 1867. For nearly two years President Andrew Johnson (Abraham Lincoln's successor) had been battling the radical Republican leadership in Congress. The radicals wanted to punish the South and treat it as a conquered province. President Johnson, on the other hand, was determined to carry out Lincoln's policies of reconciliation.

But Johnson had several factors going against him. He was from Tennessee (the only southerner in Congress who refused to secede with his state). He was also totally devoid of tact. (He could have used a Dale Carnegie course!)

Early in 1867, Congress passed a law Johnson considered an intrusion by the legislative branch of government into the executive branch. The President intentionally broke the new law to get a court test of its constitutionality. What he got instead was a vote for impeachment, the equivalent of an indictment, from the House of Representatives.

On March 5, 1867, he went on trial before the United States Senate. The radical Republicans wanted him out of the White House. Thirty-six votes (two-thirds of the Senate) were needed for conviction, and his opponents deemed any means fair to obtain that number of votes. Bribery was rampant. Of the forty-two Republican senators, six thought him innocent; thirty-five were ready to vote him guilty. Only one senator, Edmund Ross, wouldn't say how he would vote—he felt Johnson deserved a fair trial!

Ross, the freshman from Kansas, now replaced Johnson as the main actor in this melodrama. Ross had built his political career on a strong antislavery stand. Personally, he disliked Johnson—so much that the radicals had taken it for granted that he was one with them. Furious with the position he had taken, they threatened Ross with ostracism, even assassination! Ross replied that he had taken an oath to be impartial and he hoped "that I shall have the courage to vote according to the dictates of my judgment."

The Senate vote took place May 16, 1867. In his book, *Profiles in Courage,* John F. Kennedy described the scene:

> The voting tensely commenced. By the time the Chief Justice reached the name of Edmund Ross twenty-four "guilties" had been pronounced. Ten more were certain and one other practically certain. Only Ross's vote was needed to obtain the thirty-six votes necessary to convict the President. But not a single person in the room knew how this young Kansan would vote. Unable to conceal the suspense and emotion in his voice, the Chief Justice put the question to him: "Mr. Senator Ross, how say you? Is the respondent Andrew Johnson guilty or not guilty of a high misdemeanor as charged in this article?"

The room was deathly silent. Every eye stared at the freshman senator from Kansas. Sensing the mix of hopes and hatred, Ross was afraid. His throat was so dry that when he gave his answer, no one could hear him! Asked to repeat it, he spoke up loudly and unmistakably: "Not guilty!"[1]

With those two words, Ross threw away friendships, position, and fortune. His political career was over. Neither Ross nor the other six Republican senators who voted "not guilty" were ever reelected to the Senate. One American historian has called Ross's action, "The most heroic act in American history, incomparably more difficult than any deed of valor upon the field of battle."

Somehow, the idea has risen that brave people—men and women of courage—are never afraid. Nonsense! As Mark Twain expressed it, "Courage is the mastery of fear, not the absence of fear."

That was the lesson that Gideon had to learn. Gideon, like you and me, was full of both fear and faith.

For seven long years the Midianites and their allies oppressed Israel. These fierce, desert nomads would sweep down into the central part of the nation every spring "like swarms of locusts" (Judges 6:5), plundering the land of herds, crops, and fruit.

Finally, in repentance, the Israelites cried out to God. The Lord heard and raised up a deliverer—Gideon of the tribe of Manasseh.

But the angel of the Lord finds Gideon threshing wheat in a wine press. Wine presses are made for stomping grapes, not for threshing wheat. Wheat is normally beaten on a hard floor in the open air where the wind can blow away the chaff and dust.

Why is he in the wine press? Because he's afraid. He's pounding the wheat, choking on the dust, eyes red from the chaff, glancing furtively over his shoulder, keeping a watchful eye out for any Midianites who might come wandering into the area.

Then, to his surprise, he sees someone sitting under his father's oak tree. And the angel of the Lord says, "The Lord is with you, mighty warrior."

Gideon looks around, wondering, "Mighty warrior? Who's this guy talking to? Gallant? Fearless? I'm hiding in this wine press—surely he can't mean me!"

But he does.

God begins with a command and a commission: "Go in the strength you have and save Israel out of Midian's hand. Am I not sending you?" (Judges 6:14). And He makes Gideon a gracious promise: "I will be with you, and you will strike down all the Midianites together" (notice that word "together" in Judges

6:16—God will be with Gideon and act through him).

But in spite of God's promise that "together" they will pulverize the Midianites, Gideon is uncertain. He needs evidence—a sign of some kind to prove that it really is God speaking to him and not just a figment of his imagination.

Gideon is about to learn two eternal truths:

1. The *cost* of following God
2. The *courage* that is required

The cost of following God

Quickly, Gideon prepares a young goat and unleavened bread as a freewill offering for the Lord (Judges 6:19). How costly this is! After the enemy raids, food is hard to come by. The Midianite invaders have stripped the land of produce, cattle, sheep—everything they can carry off. Goats and wheat are scarce and expensive. And Gideon has a family to support (Judges 8:20).

Yet Gideon offers God the best he has. He truly "sacrifices." And as a consequence, he will never be the same.

The angel of the Lord touches the sacrifice with the tip of his staff and fire leaps forth and consumes it. Then the angel disappears. Gideon has begun to learn the cost of commitment. As the angel touched the sacrifice, so God is touching his life. Flames of opposition will arise in the next twenty-four hours. As old friends and neighbors turn against him, he will discover just how costly following the Lord can be. But he will also find that God's power and presence will enable him to walk through those fires. He has begun well.

As Gideon learned the cost of commitment, so must we. We'll never conquer the problems that beset us without totally yielding ourselves to God. With his sacrifice, Gideon says to God, "I'm yours. Whatever I have is yours. Use me for your glory."

When the sacrifice is consumed, Gideon is naturally terror-stricken. When he realizes that his visitor is an angel of the Lord, he exclaims, "Ah, Sovereign Lord! I have seen the angel of the Lord face to face!" But then the Lord speaks: "Peace! Do not be afraid. You are not going to die." (Judges 6:22, 23). Surrendering to God means peace, not judgment. So Gideon builds an altar and calls it Yahweh Shalom—the Lord is Peace. It's been a long day. But for Gideon, it isn't over yet:

> That same night the Lord said to him, "Take the second bull from your father's herd, the one seven years old. Tear down your father's altar to Baal and cut down the Asherah pole beside it. Then build a proper kind of altar to the Lord your God on the top of this height. Using the wood of the Asherah pole that you cut down, offer the second bull as a burnt offering."
>
> So Gideon took ten of his servants and did as the Lord told him. But because he was afraid of his family and the men of the town, he did it at night rather than in the daytime.
>
> Judges 6:25-27

The courage to follow God

Following the Lord is not only costly, it takes courage as well.

Israel's worship is syncretistic—a mix of worship of the true God and of false gods. Gideon's own father has an altar to Baal and an Asherah pole sitting in his front yard!

But when you choose to follow the living God, false gods have to go. There's no room for compromise, no room for accommodation, no more game-playing with God. God's men and women must purge their own hearts and homes.

Gideon tears down his father's idols, but he does it at night "because he was afraid" (Judges 6:27). Yet it takes courage for Gideon to obey God, even if it is at night. It takes courage to challenge the customs of his community and risk the fury of his father. It takes courage for Gideon to follow God, just as it does for us now.

Eddie Rickenbacker, the World War I flying ace and a recipient of the Congressional Medal of Honor once said, "Courage is doing what you're afraid to do. There can be no courage unless you're scared." Or, as someone else put it, "Courage is fear that has said its prayers."

Gideon says his prayers. Then he gets a group of ten men together and they pull down the altar to Baal and chop down the Asherah pole. In the place of these two idols, he builds an altar to the living God.

Trouble comes quickly, for any "secret" known by ten people is no secret at all! The next morning, when the men of the town discover the wreckage, they gather a lynch mob together and cry out, "Who did this?" (Judges 6:28, 29).

They soon find their man:

> When they carefully investigated, they were told, "Gideon son of Joash did it." The men of the town demanded of Joash, "Bring out your son. He must die, because he has broken down Baal's altar and cut down the Asherah pole beside it."
>
> Judges 6:29, 30

There's something contagious about courage. Like a pebble thrown into the water, Gideon's actions begin to have a ripple effect upon others. His father, Joash, had built those altars that are now just a pile of ashes and rubble. But, inspired by his son, Joash plucks up his courage and turns the mob away with a little common sense:

> "Are you going to plead Baal's cause? Are you trying to save him? Whoever fights for him shall be put to death by morning! If Baal really is a god, he can defend himself when someone breaks down his altar."
>
> Judges 6:31

Joash, in fact, is so proud of his son, that he gives him the nickname, "Jerub-Baal," which means "Baal will contend."

What is courage?

Real battles of courage occur on a daily basis. Often we don't even recognize them.

Denied permission in April of 1939 to perform in Constitution Hall because she was an African-American, contralto Marion Anderson moved to the public grounds of the Lincoln Memorial and sang to seventy-five thousand people.

Call it courage.

Serving as grand marshal of the homecoming parade at his alma mater, Michigan State, in October, 1985, Bubba Smith was distressed. The former defensive end for Michigan and the Baltimore Colts had begun appearing in beer ads in the late 1970s. Now, as he rode in the procession, students on one side of the street began to shout, "Tastes great," and students answered from the other side, "Less filling." Bubba was even more upset to see the students "drunk out of their heads" (his words) that evening at the pre-game bonfire. That night, he decided to quit making beer ads in spite of the considerable loss of income.

Call it courage.

Scott Reiter decided to be one of the 3 percent of Boy Scouts who achieve the rank of Eagle Scout. Born with spina bifida, an imperfect closure of the spinal column that leaves part of the nervous system exposed, this was no ordinary goal. For Scott, just walking was difficult. Nevertheless, he learned to hike on crutches with an eighteen-pound pack on his back. Finally, at age sixteen, he earned his long-sought Eagle rank, leading twenty-three other scouts in the planting of four hundred trees in a Southern California national forest campground.[2]

Call it courage.

Examples like these make the evening news or the morning paper. Yet other battles of real courage occur on a daily basis. The courageous are quiet. Their battles are inner. Often, we don't even recognize them.

When your toddler tumbles, then gets back up, don't call it stubbornness; call it courage.

When your teenager says "no" to a drink or a joint, and walks home from a friend's party, don't call it common sense; call it courage.

Let it be remembered that real courage is not limited to the battlefield or the Indianapolis 500 or bravely catching a thief in your house. The real tests of courage are much broader, much deeper, much quieter. They are the inner tests, like remaining faithful when nobody's looking, like enduring pain when the room is empty, like standing alone when you're misunderstood.[3]

Call it by its right name; its name is courage.

Too often we think that courage and fear never mix. As Gideon demonstrates, that just isn't true. But there are certain facts that we must realize in order to find the courage to fight the "gophers" of life.

Courage requires commitment

The call God made to Gideon—the call to courageous commitment—comes to us as well. Jesus said:

Anyone who loves his father or mother more than me is not worthy of me; anyone who loves his son or daughter more than me is not worthy of me; and anyone who does not take his cross and follow me is not worthy of me. Whoever finds his life will lose it, and whoever loses his life for my sake will find it.

Matthew 10:37-39

Jesus calls us to surrender our lives to Him. As Dietrich Bonhoeffer said, "When Jesus calls a man, He bids him come and die." He asks for all we are, all we have, all we hope to be.

But total surrender to God is more than the way to face the crises of life. As Gideon discovered, it is also the only way to peace—the only way to a relationship with Yahweh Shalom, the Lord who is Peace.

Courage brings confrontation

Courageous godliness polarizes people. The world doesn't care if we're religious and go to church, so long as we aren't really different from them. So long as we're sinfully syncretistic, building altars to Baals and Asherahs (power, money, cars, family) while mouthing prayers to God, they will let us be.

But when we courageously rip away the idols, and refuse to dilute or divide our loyalty to Christ, watch the mob gather. But there's good news.

Courage will find corroboration

Your courage will inspire others! When I served as a youth minister in west Los Angeles, one of the high school students, a young African-American named Larry, was assigned an oral report in his tenth grade biology class. They had been studying evolution, and Larry decided to make his report on the scientific evidence for creation. Imagine what courage it took to present that report at an inner city public school! But when he finished, the ripple effect began. Several students thanked him. Others said that they wished they had done a similar report. Needless to say, Larry's "stock" rose immediately.

Was Larry afraid? You'd better believe it! But he did it anyway.

As I said earlier, let's call it by its right name. It was courage.

What is courage?

John Kennedy wrote:

> To be courageous. . . requires no exceptional qualifications, no magic formula, no special combination of time, place and circumstance. It is an opportunity that sooner or later is presented to us all. . . In whatever arena of life one may meet the challenge of courage, whatever may be the sacrifices he faces if he follows his conscience—the loss of his friends, his fortune, his content-

ment, even the esteem of his fellow men—each man must decide for himself the course he will follow.[4]

What course have you chosen? If you are a Christian, you have committed to follow Jesus no matter the cost. Courage means you obey Him, even when you are afraid—especially when you're afraid.

It takes courage to deal with the challenges of life. Fear will always be with us. But the truly courageous are those who, like Gideon, Edmund Ross, Larry, and countless others, do the right and godly thing in spite of their fear.

It isn't always easy to follow Christ. He never said it would be. But we, like Gideon, have a gracious promise to rely upon: "And surely I am with you always, to the very end of the age" (Matthew 28:20).

66When a man can find no answer
he will find fear.**99**

Norman Cousins
Is Man Obsolete?

66Keep your fears to yourself;
share your courage with others.**99**

Robert Louis Stevenson

66But now, this is what the Lord says—
he who created you, O Jacob,
he who formed you, O Israel:
"Fear not, for I have redeemed you;
I have summoned you by name;
you are mine.
When you pass through the waters,
I will be with you;
and when you pass through the
rivers,
they will not sweep over you.
When you walk through the fire,
you will not be burned;
the flames will not set you ablaze.
For I am the Lord, your God,
the Holy One of Israel, your Savior.**99**

Isaiah 43:1-3

Chapter Two

Conquering Fear

On October 24, 1929 (Black Tuesday), the stock market crashed with a force that reverberates still. Within two weeks the market lay in shambles, and the United States of America plunged into the worst economic depression in its history. From 1929 through 1932, over one hundred thousand businesses failed. Over five thousand banks closed. Wages plummeted. Unemployment skyrocketed. In 1932, eleven million people (nearly 30 percent of the American work force) were searching for jobs.

The optimism of the 1920s gave way to gloom and fear.

Then a new President was elected.

On March 4, 1933, Franklin Roosevelt uttered these famous words in his inaugural address: "Let me assert my firm belief, that the only thing we have to fear is fear itself." In those immortal words, FDR declared fear, not the economy, to be Public Enemy Number One. His confidence and promise of action gave America the hope that recovery was possible.

Some fears are rooted in reality and need to be dealt with. Other fears, however, are quite irrational.

At 8:00 p.m. on October 30, 1939, Orson Welles's "Mercury Theater on the Air" was broadcast on the CBS radio airways. That night Welles and his company of players dramatized the H. G. Wells novel, *The War of the Worlds*. Using a newscast format, they reported the landing of Martians in Grovers Mill, New Jersey. The program was so realistic that panics ensued. Bars closed. Families fled their homes. Doctors and nurses called hospitals offering to help. New Jersey state troopers charged out to Grovers Mill to combat the creatures. Welles's closing words explaining the program as the Mercury Theater's "way of dressing up in a sheet and saying Boo!" did little to still the uproar. Thinking that New York City was under attack, the governor of Pennsylvania offered to send troops to New York to aid in their defense.[1]

In some ways, fear is a mixed bag. For one thing, fear isn't always harmful. It can be beneficial. God gave it to us as a survival mechanism to enable us to face the crises of life. If you catch sight of a speeding car bearing down upon you while crossing a street, fear may give you that extra surge of adrenaline that allows you to leap to safety. These are the positive values of fear; it generates caution within us and helps us avoid harm.

But there's a negative side of fear as well.

Fear can seep into our soul like an icy San Francisco fog and whisper to our heart, "What if . . . what if . . . ." Fear's apparitions bring terrors of the unknown. Its poisonous bite can paralyze its victim.

This type of fear—mixed with generous portions of worry and anxiety—can bring on physical ills (such as high blood pressure), and can even contribute to heart attacks. Living in a constant state of dread and alarm is like racing your car's engine in neutral—you're going nowhere, but using up energy and wearing out the motor. You can literally stew in your own adrenaline juice.

That kind of fear can destroy and devastate individuals, churches, and nations. It can paralyze thinking and immobilize action as the something-might-go-wrong mentality overwhelms us.

That kind of fear destroys happiness.

Irrational fears come in many different disguises. Some phobias are familiar, such as acrophobia, the fear of heights or aqua phobia, the fear of water. Others are more unusual, such as "triskaidekaphobia," the fear of the number thirteen (especially seating thirteen at a table). Certain phobias may sound silly, but they are far from amusing to those burdened by them.

From time to time, we all fall victim to some form of irrational fear: the fear of the unknown, that first day at school or on the job, your first date, speaking in front of a crowd. The fears may seem trivial, but they still exist. As Mark Twain quipped, "I don't believe in ghosts, but I'm afraid of them."

Whether real or imaginary, how can we deal with the specter of fear?

How can we conquer this enemy of peace and happiness?

Maybe we can learn some secrets from a young shepherd boy who lived three thousand years ago.

A boy named David

If anyone ever calls you a "Philistine," consider yourself insulted. In our modern terminology, the word describes an uncouth clod devoid of culture, refinement, and taste.

Originally, the Philistines came from the Island of Crete (called Caphtor in the Old Testament). After being repulsed by the Egyptians, they settled along the Eastern Mediterranean coast in about 1200 B.C. They were constantly at war with Israel.

When we meet the Philistines in 1 Samuel 17, we find them encamped on one side of the Valley of Elah, with the Israelites on the other. It was then that one of the Philistines had a bright idea—single warrior combat!

> A champion named Goliath, who was from Gath, came out
> of the Philistine camp. He was over nine feet tall. He had a
> bronze helmet on his head and wore a coat of scale armor of
> bronze weighing five thousand shekels; on his legs he wore
> bronze greaves, and a bronze javelin was slung on his back. His
> spear shaft was like a weaver's rod, and its iron point weighed six
> hundred shekels. His shield bearer went ahead of him.
>
> 1 Samuel 17:4-7

Goliath was big. Over nine feet tall in his socks, he would have made Shaquille O'Neal look like a midget, or Hulk Hogan look like a ninety-pound weakling. Goliath was strong, too. He didn't need steroids. Just wearing that 125 pounds of armor and carrying that spear, whose tip alone weighed seventeen pounds, had given him a body that would have turned the guys at Muscle Beach green with envy.

He boomed out his challenge:

> "Why do you come out and line up for battle? Am I not a Philistine, and are you not the servants of Saul? Choose a man and have him come down to me. If he is able to fight and kill me, we will become your subjects; but if I overcome him and kill him, you will become our subjects and serve us." Then the Philistine said, "This day I defy the ranks of Israel! Give me a man and let us fight each other."   1 Samuel 17:8-10

His body and his blasphemies had the desired effect: "Saul and all the Israelites were dismayed and terrified" (v. 11). Goliath wasn't the only giant stalking the Israelites that day. They were paralyzed by fear.

Every day, twice a day, for forty days, Goliath's psychological warfare worked. Fear held Saul and his soldiers in its steel grip.

But then comes day forty-one—a fateful day, indeed.

Early on that morning, Jesse sends his youngest son, David, on an errand that will prove to be a pivotal point in Jewish history. Three of David's brothers are serving at the front in Saul's army. David loads up with food for his older siblings and makes the twelve-mile hike from Bethlehem to the Valley of Elah, arriving just in time to hear Goliath's afternoon challenge. And just in time to see the Israelite's afternoon reaction: "They all ran from him in great fear." (1 Samuel 17:17-24).

Fear of others is one of the greatest hindrances we face in doing great things for God, for others, and for ourselves. In Saul we see two mistaken approaches to meeting fear:

> Now the Israelites had been saying, "Do you see how this
> man keeps coming out? He comes out to defy Israel. The king
> will give great wealth to the man who kills him. He will also give
> him his daughter in marriage and Will exempt his father's family
> from taxes in Israel." 1 Samuel 17:25

First of all, Saul is embarrassed. He isn't concerned about
God's reputation as much as his own. "His" army is being
taunted and insulted, and no one is responding. "What will
people think of me?" he wonders.

His second miscalculation is attempting to motivate his men
with material rewards—wealth, a daughter in marriage, and a
lifetime of tax exemptions. Pretty hefty rewards (I especially like
the tax exemptions!). Yet, despite the offer, for forty days no one
has done more than talk.

David, though, recognizes that Goliath is "defying" more
than the king—he is defying Israel's God. In effect, Goliath is
saying that Jehovah isn't really who He claims to be. There is a
lot more at stake than King Saul's pride, and David is shocked
and amazed at the fear that fills the camp:

> David asked the men standing near him, "What will be done
> for the man who kills this Philistine and removes this disgrace
> from Israel? Who is this uncircumcised Philistine that he should
> defy the armies of the living God?" 1 Samuel 17:26

Fear's obstacle course
Four obstacles confront David that day:

1. The contagion of fear
Fear can be as contagious as a yawn. Here are Israel's finest,
running scared. (How often has just one fearful dissenting voice,
let alone an army, killed a church's resolve to do something
great and courageous for God?).

2. The criticism of others

David's oldest brother criticizes and insults him. David is insignificant—after all, he only watches a "few sheep." Eliab attacks David's motives as well:

> When Eliab, David's oldest brother, heard him speaking with the men, he burned with anger at him and asked, "Why have you come down here? And with whom did you leave those few sheep in the desert? I know how conceited you are and how wicked your heart is; you came down only to watch the battle."
>
> 1 Samuel 17:28

3. The cautiousness of leaders

In his faithlessness and negativity, Saul discourages David:

> What David said was overheard and reported to Saul, and Saul sent for him.
>
> David said to Saul, "Let no one lose heart on account of this Philistine; your servant Will go and fight him."
>
> Saul replied, "You are not able to go out against this Philistine and fight him; you are only a boy, and he has been a fighting man from his youth."   1 Samuel 17:31-33

4. The circumstances of the situation

Saul does have a point: Goliath is big, experienced, and armed to the teeth. He is worthy of respect—and fear!

Despite these obstacles, David is determined not to be conquered by fear. While Saul and the others look only at David's exterior, God sees his inner being (1 Samuel 16:7). David may be young of age and short of stature, but he has a giant heart!

Conquering fear

How can we conquer fear? David points to three important steps:

1. Faith is the antidote for fear.

Faith isn't merely "wishful thinking." It is a vigorous trust in God.

> But David said to Saul, "Your servant has been keeping his father's sheep. When a lion or a bear came and carried off a sheep from the flock, I went after it, struck it and rescued the sheep from its mouth. When it turned on me, I seized it by its hair, struck it and killed it. Your servant has killed both the lion and the bear; this uncircumcised Philistine will be like one of them, because he has defied the armies of the living God. The Lord who delivered me from the paw of the lion and the paw of the bear will deliver me from the hand of this Philistine."
>
> 1 Samuel 17:34-37

David's faith has been honed in the wilderness. There he has killed a lion and a bear. To David, a giant seems the next logical step.

Calmness and confidence grow as we trust God's promises and follow Christ. In the daily *practice* of faith, we gain the skills and discipline necessary to face the greatest challenges of life. Time spent studying God's Word and praying arm us for the battle. The practice of our faith determines whether we cower or conquer when fear attacks.

David knows God intimately, as his psalms so clearly show. His inner shield of faith helps to keep him cool and confident in this crisis.

2. Fear cannot be defeated using the techniques and weapons of fear.

Just as David can't go into battle wearing King Saul's armor (vv. 38-40), so must we learn to rely upon God and His promises for our battles.

Goliath is insulted when "only a boy" comes out to fight him—and an apparently unarmed one at that! But David has weapons and skills that Goliath knows nothing about.

> David said to the Philistine, "You come against me with
> sword and spear and javelin, but I come against you in the name
> of the Lord Almighty, the God of the armies of Israel, whom you
> have defied. This day the Lord will hand you over to me, and I'll
> strike you down and cut off your head. . . and the whole world
> will know that there is a God in Israel. All those gathered here
> will know that it is not by sword or spear that the Lord saves; for
> the battle is the Lord's, and he will give all of you into our
> hands."   1 Samuel 17:45-47

David is armed with faith! He knows that God is in control
no matter how frightening the situation appears. That's something we need to remember: "The battle [and our future] is
the Lord's."

And so it was through faith that David was triumphant:

> So David triumphed over the Philistine with a sling and a
> stone; without a sword in his hand he struck down the Philistine
> and killed him.   1 Samuel 17:50

3. Focus on God, not circumstances.

Our tendency when afraid is to focus on ourselves—"What
if . . . what if. . . ." We worry. We're anxious. We're absorbed
with "me." David, however, is absorbed with God. Throughout
his encounter with Goliath, his focus is constantly on God's
reputation and God's honor. How we believers today need to
develop that vision! If we would focus our eyes upon God in
these waning days of the twentieth century; if we would daily
and consistently put our faith into practice, obeying God in the
small everyday battles; if we would just be caught up in His love
and His power, rather than with our problems and phobias, we,
too, could triumph over fear.

William Gladstone, one of Queen Victoria's prime ministers,
knew the power of a focus on God rather than life's difficulties.

He was once questioned as to the secret of his serenity in the face of stress and fear. He replied, "At the foot of my bed, where I can see it on retiring and on arising in the morning are the words, 'Thou wilt keep him in perfect peace, whose mind is stayed on thee: because he trusteth in thee'" (Isaiah 26:3, *King James Version*).

Perhaps you're thinking, "That all sounds well and good, but does it work today? After all, God never has done that sort of miracle in my life."

Yes, it does work today. Trusting God works as well now as it did three thousand years ago.

Please observe a key fact: nothing "miraculous" happened in 1 Samuel 17! Nothing in the account would have prevented a simpering soldier or an envious Eliab from saying, "The kid got lucky!"

Time would prove that the secret of David's life wasn't luck, but faith in the living God. As David expressed it:

> The Lord is my light and my salvation—
>> whom shall I fear?
> The Lord is the stronghold of my life—
>> of whom shall I be afraid?
>
> Psalm 27:1

Are you burdened with fears? Let Christ lift them. Enthrone Him as Lord. Focus on Him, not yourself.

> "Do not fear what they fear; do not be frightened." But in your hearts set apart Christ as Lord. 1 Peter 3: 14, 15

When my children are frightened by a nightmare, they run to me to allay their fears. Just so, we come to God in faith, for "the battle is the Lord's."

Chapter Three

Breaking the Grip of Guilt

When I was a graduate student at Pepperdine University, one of the textbooks for the Pastoral Counseling class was an interesting work by O. Hobart Mowrer. At the time he wrote *The Crisis in Psychiatry and Religion,* Mowrer was a research professor of psychology at the University of Illinois, having previously taught at Yale and Harvard. The background of his book was more fascinating than the text.

In the 1930s, Mowrer had trained as a thoroughgoing Freudian psychologist. Sigmund Freud had taught that most mental illnesses were the result of repressed sexual and hostile feelings. Too strict an upbringing, Freud contended (whether by parents or "the church"), was the cause of false feelings of guilt. In other words, Freud claimed that the neurotic had trouble, not because of any wrong he had actually done, but because others had laid false guilt on him. The cure, then, was for the neurotic "victim" to overcome his guilt feelings by giving free reign to his impulses.

Mowrer practiced what he taught. Cheating on his wife, he refused to admit or feel any guilt.

But a funny thing happened on the way to the couch. Mowrer, who was serving at the time as president of the American Psychological Association, had a nervous breakdown. And out of his recovery experience, he came to, what were to him, new conclusions that were very much at odds with accepted Freudian thought. Mowrer saw his breakdown as the result of ignoring and repudiating his conscience rather than his instincts. He concluded that in mental illness the "individual has committed tangible misdeeds, which have remained unacknowledged and unredeemed and that his anxieties thus have a realistic social basis and justification."[1] Mowrer called his new theory a "guilt theory of neurosis." By that he meant that the emotionally ill are typically burdened by real guilt, not just guilt "feelings." He spread his view widely with the 1960 publication of his book, *The Crisis in Psychiatry and Religion.*

Two definitions

Guilt. What is it? Where does it come from?

Two definitions will help clarify things as we begin our study. *Guilt* is usually defined as the feeling or sense of self-condemnation that results when we violate our moral convictions (our inner code of conduct). *Conscience,* on the other hand, is well defined by Archibald Hart in his book, *Feeling Free,* as a "God-given capacity to evaluate the rightness or wrongness of our thoughts and actions and to feel good or bad about the outcome."[2] That is, conscience is the process of thought that distinguishes good from bad, praising the one and condemning the other.

Psychologists and anthropologists have found that a conscience is common to all peoples in all cultures. (The Bible indicated this centuries ago—see Romans 2:12-15!)

God has created each of us with a conscience, and thus the capacity to feel guilt. The conscience, however, does not come preprogrammed by God with the Ten Commandments, the Sermon on the Mount, or any other set of laws. Rather, it comes with just two words emblazoned upon it:

DO RIGHT

As we grow, our parents and our culture teach us what those right and wrong actions and attitudes are. Our conscience is eventually programmed on everything from robbery to proper table etiquette. When we fail to measure up in any area, it registers on our emotions as guilt.

God's Word teaches what Mowrer found out the hard way—that guilt isn't bad. It's necessary in order to provide a "check" on individuals and societies. When functioning normally, guilt is like the flashing red light at a railroad crossing, warning of impending spiritual, emotional, or physical danger. "Stop or you will harm yourself! Don't go any further!" it screams.

Guilt, then, acting in conjunction with a healthy, well-trained conscience, helps us act responsibly.

Two extremes, however, are possible. In an incident from King David's life, we find one of these harmful extremes in operation—and discover how, in the process of healing, he avoided the other.

David's mid-life crisis

After his giant-killing exploit, David eventually becomes the second king of Israel. He is successful, both as a leader and in his personal life. His kingdom and his popularity expands during the early years of his rule (2 Samuel 5-10).

Then it hits—a mid-life crisis!

> In the spring, at the time when kings go off to war, David
> sent Joab out with the king's men and the whole Israelite army.
> They destroyed the Ammonites and besieged Rabbah. But David
> remained in Jerusalem.   2 Samuel 11:1

While his army fights at Rabbah, the Ammonite's capital city, David stays home in Jerusalem. His idleness will lead to one of the most tragic and far-reaching events in his life.

> One evening David got up from his bed and walked around
> on the roof of the palace. From the roof he saw a woman
> bathing. The woman was very beautiful.   2 Samuel 11:2

David looks, then desires, then lusts. As James 1:13-15 indicates, this is temptation's normal process:

> When tempted, no one should say, "God is tempting me."
> For God cannot be tempted by evil, nor does he tempt anyone;
> but each one is tempted when, by his own evil desire, he is
> dragged away and enticed. Then, after desire has conceived, it
> gives birth to sin; and sin, when it is full-grown, gives birth
> to death.

Allowed to go unchecked, David's smoldering lust bursts into flame. He sends for Bathsheba and they begin their adulterous affair (2 Samuel 11:3, 4).

This universe in which we live is not an accident of time plus space plus chance. It's the purposeful creation of a personal God. Therefore there are some absolutes in the area of morals and values. In his classic work, *Mere Christianity,* C. S. Lewis puts it succinctly when he says:

> I know that some people say the idea of a Law of Nature or
> decent behavior known to all men is unsound, because different
> civilizations and different ages have had quite different morali-
> ties. But this is not true. There have been differences between
> their moralities, but these have never amounted to anything like
> a total difference. If anyone will take the trouble to compare the
> moral teaching of, say, the ancient Egyptians, Babylonians,
> Hindus, Chinese, Greeks and Romans, what will really strike
> him will be how very like they are to each other and to our
> own. . . . It seems then, we are forced to believe in a real Right
> and Wrong. People may be sometimes mistaken about them,
> just as people sometimes get their sums wrong; but they are
> not a matter of mere taste and opinion any more than the mul-
> tiplication table.[3]

Guilt, then, is more than just breaking society's "dos" and "don'ts." Because this sense of right and wrong has been implanted in us by our Creator, unresolved guilt becomes a barrier that isolates and alienates, breaking relationships between God and man, as well as between men.

David's behavior with Bathsheba is a case of deliberate sin. The king was well acquainted with the Torah. He knew the Ten Commandments, yet he blatantly broke both the seventh and the tenth. And he didn't seem to "feel" guilty at all!

In counseling and study with people, I have discovered that some seem to have no conscience at all. In many cases this is due only to an underdeveloped conscience—they are, as Lewis said, mistaken about what is "decent behavior." Their need is for "training in righteousness" (2 Timothy 3:16).

But with others this apparent loss of guilt is due to a hardened conscience. When we ignore our conscience and rationalize our sins, persisting in them, we gradually become desensitized. The whisper of guilt feelings becomes fainter and fainter. In a worst-case scenario, as Paul points out in 1 Timothy 4:2, some have "seared" their consciences. The ability to feel guilt has been, in effect, burnt out of them. They refuse to take responsibility for their real sin and evil. Like the true-life murderers depicted in Truman Capote's *In Cold Blood,* who roared with laughter as they left the scene of their grisly massacre, there are no feelings of guilt or remorse.

Amazingly, David appears to have moved into the hardened state—David, the one identified in Scripture as a man after God's own heart. What went wrong? How could he, of all people, do such a thing?

Undoubtedly, it had been building for years. After all, he was the king! He could do just about anything he wanted to do. He could get just about anything he wanted to get. Over a fifteen-to twenty-year reign, he had learned to rationalize about his sin. Slowly, he had become desensitized to feelings of real guilt. Slowly, his walk with God had eroded to outer formalities. The heart he had once had for God is now a hardened rock.

But then a problem comes up. Bathsheba is pregnant (2 Samuel 11:5). "Hidden" sins have a way of showing up, don't they?

Instead of repenting and correcting the sinful relationship with courageous repentance, David tries to solve it by trickery. But his futile, clumsy attempts only cause him to sink deeper into the cesspool of deception.

Bright idea number one

David's first brainstorm is to invite Bathsheba's husband Uriah back to Jerusalem for a little "rest and relaxation," hoping that Uriah will engage in sexual relations with his wife and assume that the coming child is his own.

> So David sent this word to Joab: "Send me Uriah the Hittite." And Joab sent him to David. . . . Then David said to Uriah, "Go down to your house and wash your feet." . . . But Uriah slept at the entrance to the palace with all his master's servants and did not go down to his house.   2 Samuel 11:6, 8, 9

Uriah is no ordinary soldier. One of David's loyalist followers, one of his "mighty men," he has been with David since their wilderness adventures when they were pursued by Saul. He isn't about to engage in "R and R" while his fellow soldiers are at war:

> When David was told, "Uriah did not go home," he asked him, "Haven't you just come from a distance? Why didn't you go home?" Uriah said to David, "The ark and Israel and Judah are staying in tents, and my master Joab and my lord's men are camped in the open fields. How could I go to my house to eat and drink and lie with my wife? As surely as you live, I will not do such a thing!"   2 Samuel 11:10, 11

Bright idea number two

"Well," David figured, "if I can't get him to go home sober, maybe I can get him to go home drunk." But that brainstorm bombs as well:

> At David's invitation, he ate and drank with him, and David made him drunk. But in the evening Uriah went out to sleep on his mat among his master's servants; he did not go home.
>
> 2 Samuel 11:13

As one commentator put it, Uriah is a better man drunk than David is sober.

Bright idea number three

Kill Uriah. There seems to David only one thing left to do—arrange an "accident." David sends a note to Joab, carried by the loyal and unsuspecting Uriah:

> In it he wrote, "Put Uriah in the front line where the fighting is fiercest. Then withdraw from him so he will be struck down and die." 2 Samuel 11:15

David discovers that sin is like quicksand—the more you kick and struggle, the deeper you sink. Now he is up to his eyeballs in the slime.

David's last scheme works. Uriah dies in battle, and his "grieving" widow Bathsheba, after a "proper" period of mourning, becomes the king's newest wife. It looks as if David has tied up all the loose ends of this knotty problem. But he overlooks one important factor:

> *But the thing David had done displeased the Lord.*
>
> 2 Samuel 11:27

Shortly after the birth of a son, God sends Nathan the prophet to David with a tale of injustice guaranteed to make the king's blood boil:

> "There were two men in a certain town, one rich and the other poor. The rich man had a very large number of sheep and cattle, but the poor man had nothing except one little ewe lamb he had bought. He raised it, and it grew up with him and his children. It shared his food, drank from his cup and even slept in his arms. It was like a daughter to him.
>
> "Now a traveler came to the rich man, but the rich man refrained from taking one of his own sheep or cattle to prepare a meal for the traveler who had come to him. Instead, he took the ewe lamb that belonged to the poor man and prepared it for the one who had come to him."   2 Samuel 12:1-4

David is incensed! How can something like that happen in his kingdom? (Isn't it interesting how often the faults of others that upset us the most are the ones most similar to our own?) David is livid:

> David burned with anger against the man and said to Nathan, "As surely as the Lord lives, the man who did this deserves to die! He must pay for that lamb four times over, because he did such a thing and had no pity."
>
> 2 Samuel 12:5, 6

Then Nathan hits him between the eyes: "You are the man!" (2 Samuel 12:7).

By his actions, David has despised the many blessings God has given him (2 Samuel 12:9). Now, Nathan tells him, serious consequences are inevitable. Sin always brings consequences. Sometimes they are immediate; sometimes years pass but eventually they come. For David, the penalties are stiff: tragedy will plague his household and the child will die (2 Samuel 12:10-14).

But not all guilt is deserved. There's another extreme reaction some take to guilt. Rather than being insensitive to it, some people are overly sensitive. I love the "Garfield" cartoon that appeared a couple of years ago. Jon, Garfield's owner, is talking on the phone: "I know I haven't written yet, Mom. I'm sorry. Yes, I'll come visit you when I can, OK?" As he hangs up, he screams, "I feel like such a heel!" Garfield's comment: "Jon takes so many guilt trips, he qualifies for the frequent flyer plan."

Some of us are a lot like Jon. It's easy to make us feel guilty. We never "feel" forgiven and can never forgive ourselves. This inability to deal with guilt (whether real or imaginary) can cripple us in our relationships and make us anxious and depressed.

Dr. Archibald Hart, the head of the psychology department at Fuller Seminary, lists these qualities as symptoms of this "neurotic" guilt:

- ✔ You feel guilty nearly all the time without adequate justification.
- ✔ You continually label yourself as "bad."
- ✔ Your guilt reactions last a long time.
- ✔ Your guilt reactions to little wrongs are extreme.
- ✔ Your guilt so incapacitates you that you cannot relate to anyone and want to be alone.
- ✔ You cannot stop remembering all your past misdeeds.[4]

David's reaction to his sin can teach us how to avoid this extreme and break the grip of guilt.

David sees himself as he truly is—a guilty sinner: "Then David said to Nathan, 'I have sinned against the Lord.'" (2 Samuel 12:13). No excuses. No rationalizations. He simply confesses and admits his guilt.

And God forgives him!

Nathan replied, "The Lord has taken away your sin. You are not going to die" (2 Samuel 12:13).

Amazing grace! According to the Law, David deserves to die on the counts of murder and adultery (Leviticus 20:10; 24:17). But God forgives him. Highlight that truth!

Too many Christians find it difficult to apply God's grace to themselves. Some of us live in the past, running a constant video tape of our sins through our mind's eye. Others list their sins in a "rank order" and can apply God's grace to the "little ones" but not the big ones.

David's experience warns us to avoid one extreme of the guilt spectrum. Never become insensitive to your sin: "So, if you think you are standing firm, be careful that you don't fall!" (1 Corinthians 10:12). No one is immune to sin—not kings, not elders, not preachers (as the tele-evangelist scandals of the 1980s so painfully demonstrated). Past victories can't see us through the future.

But David also gives us hope for the other extreme. We can be forgiven! David coveted. He stole. He committed adultery. He lied. He murdered. What have you or I done that's worse than that?

David confronted his sin, confessed it and turned from it. He poured out his remorse in a psalm of prayer to the Lord:

> Have mercy on me, O God,
>   according to your unfailing love;
>   according to your great compassion
>   blot out my transgressions.
> Wash away all my iniquity
>   and cleanse me from my sin.
>
>   . . . .
>
> Create in me a pure heart, O God,
>   and renew a steadfast spirit within me.
>
>   . . . .
>
> Save me from bloodguilt, O God,
>   the God who saves me,
>   and my tongue will sing of your righteousness.
>   Psalm 51:1, 2, 10, 14

David's entire prayer of confession is recorded in Psalm 51. It's valuable reading for a guilty heart.

How can we break guilt's grip?

Our first need is to heal the broken relationship sin creates between us and God (Romans 3:23-25). No matter how sordid the past may be, God can make us new. No matter how mixed up our life was or is, He can cleanse us, and point us in a new direction. Jesus is the only final answer to real guilt. Come to Him in faith.

But those of us who are already children of God also may be burdened by guilt. Break free of guilt's bonds. The following suggestions will help:

1. Accept the fact that consequences often do result from past sins. Terrible events were unleashed because of David's sin, but those consequences didn't mean he wasn't forgiven (underline again in your Bible 2 Samuel 12:13).

2. Confess your wrong and turn from it in repentance. If possible, make restitution and rebuild relationships. Sincerely ask God to forgive you.

3. Take God at His Word. Claim the promise of 1 John 1:9 (it is, after all, addressed to Christians):

> If we confess our sins, he is faithful and just and will forgive us our sins and purify us from all unrighteousness.

Accept the forgiveness God has promised:

> He does not treat us as our sins deserve
> or repay us according to our iniquities.
> For as high as the heavens are above the earth,
> so great is his love for those who fear him;
> as far as the east is from the west,
> so far has he removed our transgressions from us.
>
> Psalm 103:10-12

4. Reclaim God's promise if you recall past sins and guilt. It is Satan who loves to keep us on that merry-go-round of guilt, acting as if we are not forgiven when our memories attack. Rather than ask God's forgiveness once again for sins that you have already repented of, reclaim the reality of your forgiveness. Pray, "Thank You, Lord for the fact that You have forgiven me!"

5. And always remember—no situation is hopeless. Paul Jordan writes in *A Man's Man Called by God*:

> If David and Bathsheba had been in one of our twentieth century churches, they would probably have been drummed out of the corps. But God doesn't work that way in people's lives. He forgives and then blesses those who have sinned. If he didn't, there would be no hope for any of us.[5]

Does God really forgive and bless sinners?

Absolutely. There seems to have been a special love between David and Bathsheba in their marriage. And, though their first child dies, a second, Solomon, is later born to them (2 Samuel 12:24). And through that union came the One who was to bless all mankind—Jesus, the Messiah!

> Amazing grace! how sweet the sound,
> That saved a wretch like me!
> I once was lost, but now am found,
> Was blind, but now I see.[6]
> —John Newton

Don't rationalize real guilt or sin. Deal with it quickly through repentance and confession. But never allow past, forgiven sin to strangle you. As Will Rogers said, "Don't let yesterday use up too much of today."

God wants to forgive you and bless you. Let Him!

"You keep carryin' that anger,
it'll eat you up inside.**"**

Don Henley
"The Heart of the Matter"

"Get rid of all bitterness, rage and
anger, brawling and slander, along with
every form of malice. Be kind and
compassionate to one another,
forgiving each other, just as in
Christ God forgave you.**"**

Ephesians 4:31, 32

Chapter Four

Wrestling With Resentment

It was ironic that he had a bachelor's degree in sociology. Sociologists are supposed to help people. But he carried a grudge against society. The bumper sticker on his car read, "I'm not deaf, I'm just ignoring you."

The few people who knew him found him sullen and full of unfocused anger. "Always ready to get even with something," was how one expressed it. His fuse was ignited when he lost his welder's job, and subsequently his home, in Massillon, Ohio.

He packed up his grudge, his wife, and his two daughters and moved to southern California in January, 1984. He eventually found a job as a condominium security guard, but was fired that July.

His inner bomb finally exploded on Wednesday, July 18.

The day before, he had called a mental-health clinic and left a message on their answering machine. His call was never returned.

After an appearance in traffic court, he took his family to lunch at McDonald's. That afternoon they spent some time at the San Diego Zoo. They were looking at the animals when he turned to his wife and said, "Society had their chance."

Late that afternoon, at their apartment, he kissed his wife good-bye.

She asked if he needed any money.

He shook his head. "I'm going hunting," he said, "hunting for humans."

Then James Huberty drove down the block to McDonald's in San Ysidro. He shot twenty-two people to death and wounded another seventeen, before the police finally killed him. It was the largest one-day mass murder in the history of the United States.

Why would anyone do something like that? What possessed James Huberty on that summer day in 1984?

As the media tried to make some sense of it, one psychologist, interviewed by *Time* magazine, commented that random, serial murderers share one characteristic: "a deep, suppressed rage."[1]

James Alan Fox, a professor of criminal justice at Northeastern University and author of *Mass Murder: America's Growing Menace,* said most mass murderers "aren't lunatics. They don't hear voices. They're not psychotic. They're angry, bitter, desperate, maladjusted—but not insane."[2]

Rage. Hate. Resentment. Bitterness.

Our world seems to be caught up in a wave of hostility. The major acts of violence—murder, assault, rape, global wars—make the evening news. But the thousands of smaller acts of rage—the resentments and hostilities each of us struggles with, the bitterness and anger that tear apart friendships, destroy families, and torpedo careers—these rarely make headlines.

Resentment is like a volcano in the soul. If we allow it to heat up, if we brood on it and let the pressure mount, it's only a matter of time before it explodes like Mount St. Helens.

The damage is always tragic and often irreparable. A shattered marriage. A battered child. The loss of a job. An alcoholic stupor.

Resentment.

Have you ever found yourself saying:

"He'll be sorry he did that to me."

"I don't think I can ever forgive her for saying that."

"I should have gotten that promotion. It's just not fair!"

At one time or another, we've all said or thought such words. No one is immune.

How can we overcome the monster of resentment?

How can we turn down the heat under the anger simmering in our hearts?

Resentment's downward spiral

In Genesis 37, we meet Jacob and his large brood living in Canaan. Their story graphically recounts how resentment fractured a family, and it suggests ways to deal with this problem.

> Joseph, a young man of seventeen, was tending the flocks
> with his brothers, the sons of Bilhah and the sons of Zilpah,
> his father's wives, and he brought their father a bad report
> about them.   Genesis 37:2

In Joseph's deteriorating relationship with his brothers, we discover the downward spiraling steps of resentment.

Step number one: think about it

The root cause of resentment lies in mishandled anger. Training in the handling of that volatile emotion begins in the home. Unfortunately for Jacob's sons, they learned a number of bad habits from their parents. They grew up watching their father Jacob and their grandfather Laban deceive each other. They observed the bitter rivalry between Leah and Rachel. Two of the brothers, Levi and Simeon, had well-earned reputations for anger and violence, having slaughtered all the male inhabitants of a nearby town (Genesis 34:25).

Now Joseph tattles on four of them (Dan and Naphtali the sons of Bilhah, and Gad and Asher, the sons of Zilpah), and those four aren't about to forget it.

That's how resentment starts, isn't it? Someone says something offensive about us (we might even deserve the comment) and we resent it. We begin to nurse a grudge, and the offense begins constantly to prey on our thoughts. The background of the English word "resentment" reflects the process. It comes from the Latin word *resento* and carries the idea, "to re-feel. In resentment we re-feel the agony and hurt of previous experiences.

The more we focus on the hurt, the more we re-feel it and look for excuses to continue feeding it. (When you are looking for reasons to hate, they are easy enough to find):

> Now Israel loved Joseph more than any of his other sons,
> because he had been born to him in his old age; and he made a
> richly ornamented robe for him. When his brothers saw that
> their father loved him more than any of them, they hated him.
>
> Genesis 37:3, 4

So, Joseph is daddy's little pet! The older brothers' anger at this favoritism quickly settles into jealousy and hate, leading them to the next step in resentment's decent.

Step number two: talk about it

After the simmering grudge comes verbal hostility: "and [they] could not speak a kind word to him." (Genesis 37:4). Their bitterness and hate spills out of their mouths.

Joseph, being something of a tactless teenager at this stage of his life, doesn't help the situation. When he relates his dreams at the breakfast table about sheaves of grain bowing to his sheaf, and the sun, moon and stars bowing before him, he only adds fuel to the fire (Genesis 37:5-11). His brothers gag on their oatmeal. Their reaction is predictable:

"And they hated him all the more because of his dream and what he had said" (Genesis 37:8). They are angry and jealous (Genesis 37:11). This led to the final step in resentment's spiral.

Step number three: take action on it

The last step is vengeance. Joseph is sent by his father to

check up on his brothers (Genesis 37:12-17). Unfortunately for Joseph, his beautiful coat was like waving a red flag in front of a bull:

> But they saw him in the distance, and before he reached them, they plotted to kill him.
>
> "Here comes that dreamer!" they said to each other. "Come now, let's kill him and throw him into one of these cisterns and say that a ferocious animal devoured him. Then we'll see what comes of his dreams."
>
> Genesis 37:18-20

The cost of resentment

Resentment—leading to the urge to get even—is a giant we all wrestle. Some people are proud of it. Perhaps you've seen a car with the bumper sticker that reads, "I don't get mad, I get even." (Personally, I steer as far away from one of those as possible!) But there is a high cost to resentment.

The physical cost

In his fascinating book, *None of These Diseases,* Dr. S. I. McMillen wrote, "What a person eats is not as important as the bitter spirit, the hates, and the feelings of guilt that eat at him. A dose of baking soda in the stomach will never reach these acids that destroy body, mind, and soul."[3]

Our body pays for our grudges and our hates. The cost is high—skyrocketing blood pressure, strokes, heart attacks, colitis—the list goes on and on. Resentment is a killer. According to Alcoholics Anonymous, the number-one cause of death among alcoholics is resentment.

Dr. McMillen relates the story of Dale Carnegie's visit to Yellowstone National Park. One of the park guides explained that the grizzly bear could whip any other animal except perhaps the Kodiak bear and the buffalo. When a grizzly is feeding from a garbage can, there's no way that he'll let any other animal eat with him—with one exception: the skunk. The grizzly bear could easily win a fight with a skunk. He probably resents the striped pest muscling in on his lunch. Why doesn't he just stomp the little rascal?

Because he knows the high cost of getting even!

As Carnegie points out, grizzly bears are smarter than many humans.[4]

Few of us get even with a gun like James Huberty did in San Ysidro. Few seek vengeance like David Burke, the fired passenger agent who shot his former boss and the flight crew on a PSA flight in December, 1987, causing Burke and forty-three other passengers to plunge thirty thousand feet to their deaths.

No, those methods are unscriptural (as well as being illegal). So what do we do?

We get verbal. We collect supporters who "console" us and feed our grudges by reminding us how wronged we've been.

Of course, bitter verbal attacks aren't scriptural either, but they do have the advantage of keeping us off death row. Yet, even verbal hostility can harm us.

Dr. Redford Williams, a professor of psychiatry at Duke University, has said, "We have strong evidence that hostility alone damages the heart. It's the anger. It sends your blood pressure skyrocketing. It provokes your body to create unhealthy chemicals. For hostile people, anger is a poison."[5]

There is a physical cost of resentment!

The mental and spiritual cost

Dr. McMillen writes:

> The moment I start hating a man, I become his slave. I can't enjoy my work any more because he even controls my thoughts. My resentments produce too many stress hormones in my body and I become fatigued after only a few hours of work. The work I formerly enjoyed is now drudgery. . . . The man I hate hounds me wherever I go. I can't escape his tyrannical grasp on my

mind. When the waiter serves me porterhouse steak with French fries, asparagus, crisp salad, and strawberry shortcake smothered with ice cream, it might as well be stale bread and water. My teeth chew the food and I swallow it, but the man I hate will not permit me to enjoy it.[6]

Joseph's oldest brother talks the others out of murder, but they take their vengeance by selling him into slavery (Genesis 37:23-28). They then deceive their father, leading him to believe that Joseph has been devoured by wild animals (Genesis 37:31-35).

But when we seek vengeance, guilt moves in. Joseph's brothers carried theirs for twenty years. How do we know that their guilt never left them? It was a long time coming, but eventually Joseph rose to become Pharaoh's right-hand man. When a famine struck Egypt and Canaan, his brothers came down to Egypt to buy food. They didn't realize that the Egyptian they were dealing with was their kid brother, Joseph!

To discover whether or not they had had a change of heart in the intervening years, Joseph accused them of being spies. Guess what their reaction was:

> They said to one another, "Surely we are being punished because of our brother. We saw how distressed he was when he pleaded with us for his life, but we would not listen; that's why this distress has come upon us."
>
> Genesis 42:21

Guilt! Resentment carries a fearful mental and spiritual price tag.

Resentment's source

Resentment. Hate. Bitterness. Hostility. Vengeance. We know that these attitudes are forbidden in Scripture, when we read about the "acts of the sinful nature" in Galatians 5:20, 21 and in other lists of sins. Where do these feelings and attitudes come from? How can we overcome them?

Primarily, they are the result of mishandled anger. Since anger is an emotion, it is neither right or wrong in itself. Rather, its use or misuse makes it either positive or destructive. Anger is dangerous because it can so easily run to excess. Perhaps that's why there are so many warnings about it in Scripture:

> My dear brothers, take note of this: Everyone should be
> quick to listen, slow to speak and slow to become angry, for
> man's anger does not bring about the righteous life that
> God desires.   James 1:19, 20

Because of warnings such as this, some have argued that we should never get angry. They say that anger is a sin in itself. However, you've probably found as I have, that anger is impossible to prevent. The real issue is not "how to prevent anger" but "what to do with anger when it comes."

In his book, *Communication—The Key to Your Marriage,* psychologist Norman Wright suggests that there are four ways we deal with anger.

(1) Some repress it.

They force it down into their subconscious and force. . . themselves . . . not . . . to . . . think . . . about. . . it. This repression often has severe consequences, however, the anger can turn in on us, causing depression.

(2) Others try to suppress it.

They try to consciously hold the lid on the boiling cauldron of their anger and bitterness. That causes resentment. Like James Huberty, the person is a human time bomb just waiting to explode.

(3) Others express it.

They "blow up." They explode and break things (sometimes people).

This was the method I learned as a child and carried into my adult years. My wife and I had been married only a few months when she said something that really ticked me off. I can't remember what it was but I still remember what I did. I stomped off and, in my rage, struck the back of an old wooden chair. The back flopped down as if it were on hinges.

This style of expressing anger is both destructive and costly!

(4) The wisest confess it.

Deal with it and develop a new way of looking at life and at anger-producing situation:

> "In your anger do not sin": Do not let the sun go down while you are still angry, and do not give the devil a foothold.
>
> Ephesians 4:26, 27

In other words, be honest about your anger. Confess it to yourself and to God, and get in touch with your feelings. Deal with it as quickly as possible. Don't nurse it; that gives Satan a foot in the door of your heart. When you don't allow yourself to feel it and deal with it, anger turns into bitterness and resentment, which easily progress to hate and violence.[7]

> Get rid of all bitterness, rage and anger, brawling and slander, along with every form of malice.
>
> Ephesians 4:31

How can we overcome resentment?

(1) Begin with prevention, with the proper handling of your anger. Be honest with yourself about your emotions and deal with anger quickly!

But what if it's too late? What if you've already got a bundle of hate, bitterness, and resentment twisting your stomach into a pretzel? What then?

(2) Pray for those you hate. "Pray for those who persecute you," Jesus said (Matthew 5:44). Years ago, I felt I was being

treated unfairly by one of the elders at my church. My heart was filled with resentment until I began to obey Jesus in this area. I discovered that it's hard to hate someone when you're praying for him.

(3) Practice active love toward the one you resent. We can't always change our feelings, but we can change our response. When Jesus said, "Love your enemies" (Matthew 5:44) He wasn't talking about feelings, but actions. The apostle Paul put it this way:

> "If your enemy is hungry, feed him; if he is thirsty, give him something to drink. In doing this, you will heap burning coals on his head. Do not be overcome by evil, but overcome evil with good." Romans 12:20, 21

What sort of actions might love take? Try a compliment or a note of encouragement. Hard? Absolutely—but acting in love and kindness can transform hate into love. Edwin Markham, in his short poem, "Outwitted," described the process:

> He drew a circle that shut me out
> Heretic, rebel, a thing to flout.
> But Love and I had the wit to win:
> We drew a circle that took him in.

(4) Remember two great truths. Remember that God has forgiven you. "Be kind and compassionate to one another, forgiving each other, just as in Christ God forgave you" (Ephesians 4:32). When we remember how God has been merciful to us, we are empowered to forgive others.

Remember that God is still sovereign and in control. No matter what others have done to us, God's promise still applies:

> And we know that in all things God works for the good of those who love him, who have been called according to his purpose. Romans 8:28

It worked that way for Joseph. When his brothers found that their Egyptian lord was Joseph, they were terrified (Genesis 45:3). Then he told them his secret—the secret that can turn hate into love:

> "And now, do not be distressed and do not be angry with yourselves for selling me here, because it was to save lives that God sent me ahead of you. . . . God sent me ahead of you to preserve for you a remnant on earth and to save your lives by a great deliverance.
>
> "So then, it was not you who sent me here, but God."
>
> Genesis 45:5, 7, 8

Ultimately, Joseph's secret for love and forgiveness lay in his certainty that God was in control.

Years later, when Jacob died, Joseph's brothers panicked. They assumed that Joseph was secretly nursing a grudge and would now pay them back since their father was dead (Genesis 50:15). Joseph's reaction? He wept. Then he said:

> "Don't be afraid. Am I in the place of God? You intended to harm me, but God intended it for good to accomplish what is now being done, the saving of many lives."
>
> Genesis 50:19, 20

Recognizing that God loves us and is in control of the universe sets us free to love and forgive.

In conclusion

Wrestle with resentment. Overcome it. Learn how to properly handle anger—feel it and deal with it. Pray for your enemies, treat them lovingly, and always remember, God is still on His throne. He loves us and has forgiven us. How can we do less for others?

"For if you forgive men when they sin against you, your heavenly father will also forgive you. But if you do not forgive men their sins, your Father will not forgive your sins."

Matthew 6:14, 15

Booker T. Washington said, "I will not let any man reduce my soul to the level of hate." Not a bad way for all of us to live. I think Joseph would agree.

Chapter Five

Dealing with Depression

Their photographs leaped from the front page of my newspaper—smiling, happy faces. Haunting faces.

David Engel had graduated from the University of Wisconsin with a nearly 4.0 grade point average in the field of mechanical engineering. His failure to get a perfect GPA would haunt him for many years. After working for Texas Instruments, he found a job with a smaller company at the salary of fifty thousand dollars a year—a sizable sum in the late 1970s.

Everything seemed to be going great. With a wife and two daughters, Engel appeared to have the perfect family. They owned a beautiful home in Torrance, California, rental property in Manhattan Beach, and a time-share interest in a San Diego ranch resort. David Engel was active at his Rolling Hills church, playing on its volleyball and softball teams and serving as the chairman of the pre-school committee.

Then a financial crisis hit. He lost his job because the small firm couldn't afford his salary any longer. For several months he was unemployed. Depression set in and he began seeing a psychologist for counseling. At last he found work with a firm in El Segundo, but at a 20 percent cut in pay from his old wage.

David Engel was forty-one years old.

He took a detailed, mid-life self-examination and gave himself straight F's. It was November. He was facing large mortgage payments on his homes. Property taxes were due December 10 and Christmas was coming. The financial strain was too great. Just before Thanksgiving he had a mental breakdown. He became suicidal. His psychologist arranged to have him hospitalized, then dropped the plan when Engel seemed to improve. On November 28, he visited his psychologist who noted his condition as "normal but mildly depressed."

The next day, on the way home from work, David Engel bought a twenty-gauge Winchester shotgun in a sporting goods store. It was on sale—only $138.44. That night, during the Johnny Carson show, he wrote the following:

> I guess you are supposed to leave a note, so here it is. I am just plain tired. I have received all the help and support one could ask for. I feel I got financially too far behind at my age to provide for my family in an adequate way. Too many things need fixing and replacing. I see two difficult years ahead. . . . Too many changes. No stability. We provide very little opportunity in our society to make a change without great financial penalty.[1]

Then he walked methodically from room to room and killed his wife, his seven and four-year-old daughters, and finally, himself.

Depression

Once upon a time, you had hopes and dreams for success in your chosen field, or for a beautiful home, or for a happy marriage, or for a large income. Then it all fell apart. A feeling of helplessness set in. The situation seemed to be beyond your powers of coping.

I know. I've been there. We all have, to one degree or another.

Most depression is a reaction to some kind of loss. It may be the loss of a spouse through death or divorce, the loss of a job, or something less tangible (yet still very real), like the loss of reputation or self-esteem.

Depression can spawn physical ills—headaches, weight loss

or gain, insomnia, fatigue, impotence.

The National Institute of Mental Health has estimated that 20 percent of the American public have significant symptoms of depression. The cost to the economy is estimated at four billion dollars a year in lost work hours and medical bills. The social cost is even higher, measured in broken marriages, troubled children, and suicides.

Every day in the United States about fifty-five people kill themselves—over twenty thousand a year. For every suicide, ten attempt it. In *Depression: Finding Hope and Meaning in Life's Darkest Shadow,* Dr. Emery Nester writes: "It is unlikely that suicide will occur in isolation from depression. . . . Suicide is associated with feelings of despair."[2]

Depression strikes all strata of our society, the rich and the poor, the famous and the unknown, the intelligent and the average, Christians and non-Christians. Those in the helping professions—nurses, teachers, and ministers—seem especially prone.

Here is how one believer described it:

> Depression is
> It really is.
> You can't get away from it,
> Except temporarily,
> For it returns
> Like a cat creeping
> Upon its prey.
> It undermines the ambition,
> Saps the vitality,
> And weakens emotional stability.
> You are always thinking,
> And you wonder.
> What is the use?
> How can I get rid of it?
> When will it end?
> Then one day,

You suddenly realize—
It's gone!
I'm free!
But, back in the deep
Recesses of the mind,
There is the thought—
How long until
It strikes again?
                    Jean Galloway[3]

What can we do about this enemy of happiness? How can we deal with depression?

Elijah sings the blues

"Elijah was a man just like us. He prayed earnestly" (James 5:17). Elijah—a man like me? Elijah? The guy who didn't die, but was so close to God that he went to Heaven in a whirlwind and a fiery chariot?

Elijah was a man of prayer, but he also got deeply depressed. A "man just like us."

When we pick up his story in 1 Kings 19, he is fresh from the greatest spiritual triumph of his illustrious career—the defeat of the four hundred fifty prophets of Baal on Mount Carmel. Fire from the Lord had fallen and consumed his sacrifices—even the water in the trench around the offerings had been vaporized. The Israelites had cried out, "Yahweh—He is God." The false prophets had been slain. King Ahab had been suitably impressed. Elijah's expectations and hopes for a national revival were high.

After a word of encouragement to King Ahab regarding the end of the drought, Elijah runs ahead of the King's chariot the twenty miles back to Jezreel. He is supporting Ahab, demonstrating his loyalty. He knows Ahab has to face his wife, Queen Jezebel! But Elijah was certain the events of that day would put some starch in Ahab's spine.

But that isn't how it worked out:

> Now Ahab told Jezebel everything Elijah had done and how
> he had killed all the prophets with the sword. So Jezebel sent a
> messenger to Elijah to say, "May the gods deal with me, be it
> ever so severely, if by this time tomorrow I do not make your life
> like that of one of them."
>
> Elijah was afraid and ran for his life.
>
> 1 Kings 19:1-3

Elijah's hopes are dashed. Jezebel will not repent. So Elijah panics and runs.

Now isn't that interesting? He has just wiped out four hundred fifty false prophets and now he runs from one woman. He loses his perspective and falls into the "black hole" of depression. He definitely is a "man just like us."

He nearly becomes suicidal.

> He. . . went a day's journey into the desert. He came to a broom
> tree, sat down under it and prayed that he might die. "I have
> had enough, Lord," he said. "Take my life; I am no better than
> my ancestors."   1 Kings 19:4

What causes depression?

Often, depression follows a "mountaintop" experience. It is, in fact, almost a predictable pattern: our emotional highs are followed by emotional lows. Expect a letdown. Periodic lows are normal.

Depression often follows intense stress and activity like Elijah experienced on Mount Carmel. Some have called it the "post adrenaline blues." That's the reason someone once advised preachers never to resign on Monday!

Depression often coincides with physical and emotional exhaustion. As a youth minister, every year in late August I would consider leaving the ministry. I wondered why. After this

annual depression occurred several years in a row, I finally figured it out: I was just plain exhausted after a summer of mission
trips, camps, and countless other youth activities! Realizing that
connection helped me survive that annual collapse.

Depression often follows deep disappointment or loss. Elijah
had expected national repentance led by the king. Then his
hopes were destroyed.

Anger is another ingredient of the depression stew. But it's an
anger that's turned inward. Elijah was angry over his loss of
hope. Who did he blame? "I'm no better than my ancestors."
He had given himself to God's work. He had done his best. Yet
he blamed himself! That's the way depression is.

How does God help Elijah?

To help Elijah deal with and overcome his depression, God
takes steps that we can observe and copy.

1. God provides sorely needed food and rest

The Lord has created us as physical, psychological, and spiritual beings. Trouble in one of these areas can affect the others.
The cause of depression can be physical—for instance, a thyroid
disorder or hypoglycemia.

The first thing God prescribes for Elijah is food and rest:

> Then he lay down under the tree and fell asleep.
>
> All at once an angel touched him and said, "Get up and eat."
> He looked around, and there by his head was a cake of bread
> baked over hot coals, and a jar of water. He ate and drank and
> then lay down again.
>
> The angel of the Lord came back a second time and touched
> him and said, "Get up and eat, for the journey is too much for
> you." So he got up and ate and drank. Strengthened by that
> food, he traveled forty days and forty nights until he reached
> Horeb, the mountain of God.
>
> 1 Kings 19:5-8

2. Next, God counsels Elijah

Therapy session number one begins:

> And the word of the Lord came to him: "What are you doing
> here, Elijah?"
>
> He replied, "I have been very zealous for the Lord God
> Almighty. The Israelites have rejected your covenant, broken
> down your altars, and put your prophets to death with the
> sword. I am the only one left, and now they are trying to kill
> me too."
>
> The Lord said, "Go out and stand on the mountain in the
> presence of the Lord, for the Lord is about to pass by."
>
> Then a great and powerful wind tore the mountains apart
> and shattered the rocks before the Lord, but the Lord was not in
> the wind. After the wind there was an earthquake, but the Lord
> was not in the earthquake. After the earthquake came a fire, but
> the Lord was not in the fire. And after the fire came a gentle
> whisper.   1 Kings 19:9-12

In this first therapy session, God lets Elijah share his feelings
openly and honestly. In the book he co-authored with Dr.
Nester, Don Baker relates his personal struggle with depression.
Baker writes, "A depressed person needs desperately to hear
himself."[4] God gives Elijah that opportunity. Notice what the
Lord doesn't say. He doesn't say, "Come on, fella, cheer up.
Don't feel that way." A depressed person isn't ready to respond
to that approach. Instead, God lets Elijah vent his anger with his
"poor-me-what-have-I-done-to-deserve-this?" speech.

Elijah doesn't need someone to give him advice. He needs
someone to listen to him. As Sidney Jourard reveals in his book,
The *Transparent Self,* no one can really know himself until he
has been able to disclose and verbalize himself to someone he
can trust.[5]

Elijah also needs a fresh view of God. Elijah is familiar with
earthquakes, winds, and fires. That's the kind of prophet he is!
But a still, small voice? That's altogether new and refreshing.

We, like Elijah, need to listen to the Lord in the stillness of prayer and meditation as well as in the activity of ministry! God then launches into therapy session number two:

> When Elijah heard it, he pulled his cloak over his face and went out and stood at the mouth of the cave.
>
> Then a voice said to him, "What are you doing here, Elijah?"
>
> He replied, "I have been very zealous for the Lord God Almighty. The Israelites have rejected your covenant, broken down your altars, and put your prophets to death with the sword. I am the only one left, and now they are trying to kill me too."
>
> The Lord said to him, "Go back the way you came, and go to the Desert of Damascus. When you get there, anoint Hazael king over Aram. Also, anoint Jehu son of Nimshi king over Israel, and anoint Elisha son of Shaphat from Abel Meholah to succeed you as prophet. . . Yet I reserve seven thousand in Israel—all whose knees have not bowed down to Baal and all whose mouths have not kissed him."   1 Kings 1 9:13-16, 18

God is very patient with Elijah! First, the Lord helps him get in touch with his feelings, then He helps him get in touch with reality. Depression distorts our view of reality. It draws ridiculous conclusions in its search for the cause of its despair. It cries out, "I need a divorce. . . I need a new job. . ." It sees only the negative. It forgets and overlooks the positive. Little problems look like Mount Everest, and temptations and struggles appear endless.

In his despair, Elijah forgets about his friend, Obadiah, and the one hundred prophets of God who have been hidden and protected (1 Kings 18:4). God reminds him that he isn't expected to lead Israel all by himself. Hazael, Jehu, and Elisha will help him. (Many ministers and Christian workers need to hear that message today!) Elijah isn't the only "true believer." There are still seven thousand who haven't worshiped Baal.

Let's be honest and admit that believers in these days of the

New Covenant, as in the days of the Old, do get depressed.

There are several different types of depression (such as psychotic and manic-depressive), but the most common is reactive depression. It is so named because it is caused by our reaction to significant losses or changes in our environment and circumstances. With it comes anger turned in on ourselves.

We need to get some myths and misconceptions out of our minds and out of our churches.

Myth number one

Some Christians say, "It's a sin to be depressed." Depression is not a sin! It might be caused by sin, but in and of itself, it is not sin. It may, in fact, be a normal, healthy response, as in the death of a loved one. God never laid a guilt trip on Elijah.

Myth number two

Others say, "Spiritual Christians don't get depressed." If you want to heap more depression on someone, that's a good line to use. Only a perfect person would never get depressed. Many strong believers, like the well-known, nineteenth-century preacher, Charles Spurgeon, have had constant struggles with depression.

Depression lowers our mood level, but not necessarily our faith.

Depression is a feeling. It's neither right nor wrong. It's just there. What we do with our feelings makes them right or wrong.

Feelings are part of being human. We need to understand and get in touch with our feelings—especially anger. But don't believe all of your feelings. Many are quite irrational, as Elijah discovered.

Dealing with depression

How can we best deal with depression? Here are several suggestions, based upon God's dealing with Elijah:

1. Begin with your physical health. Eat a good, nutritional diet and get plenty of rest and exercise. Have a physical examination if depression is chronic.

2. Verbalize your feelings and frustrations to God. He loves you, and He will listen. Keep an open channel of prayer.

3. Face reality and rediscover a proper perspective. Don't let tough times and negative emotions cancel out the positive memories of the past. Be sure to get all the facts. See the big picture—there's a light at the end of the tunnel.

4. Expose yourself to God's "gentle whisper." I know from personal experience how difficult it is to read God's Word and pray when depression blankets your soul. But it's necessary to fill ourselves with the Bible's crystal truths in order to counter the lies and distortions of despair's "black hole."

5. Take your eyes off self and put them back upon God. Elijah lost sight of God's presence and power. He thought everything was up to him. But God has never depended upon any one person to accomplish His plans. Keep your eyes on the Lord.

6. Get busy. Common advice counselors give the depressed is to "Get active, find a hobby, do something!" That was God's advice to Elijah. In essence, He told him, "There's still something for you to do. Your life still has meaning."

7. Finally, find a friend. We weren't made to live in isolation. Christians are part of a community of love and fellowship, Christ's body, His church. We need each other, just as Elijah needed Elisha to share his dreams and ministry:

> So Elijah went from there and found Elisha son of Shaphat. He was plowing with twelve yoke of oxen, and he himself was driving the twelfth pair. Elijah went up to him and threw his cloak around him.
>
> . . .
>
> So Elisha . . . set out to follow Elijah and became his attendant.   1 Kings 19:19, 21

"And we know that in all things God works for the good of those who love him, who have been called according to his purpose." That's the tremendous promise of Romans 8:28.

Look for the meaningful benefits in all the events of life— even in depression. What kind of good can God bring from depression? We learn more about ourselves. We become better equipped to minister to other sufferers "so that we can comfort those in any trouble with the comfort we ourselves have received from God" (2 Corinthians 1:4). He molds us into Christ's image as we grow through tragedy and loss. Depression can be used by God to help us grow spiritually.

We've all faced times in the black hole.

We've all asked in moments of despair and tragedy, "Is that all there is to life?"

Jesus Christ is in the business of changing lives: "Therefore, if anyone is in Christ, he is a new creation; the old has gone, the new has come!" (2 Corinthians 5:17).

Elijah was "a man just like us"—and he battled depression.

But, with God's help, he dealt with it and overcome it. And we can too!

Chapter Six

Hope for Hostile Hearts

It was a hot summer evening, July 18, 1987. Albert Morgan, a roofer who lived in Santa Ana, California, was angry and frustrated. He and his wife were inching their way down the Costa Mesa Freeway trying to get to the Orange County Fairgrounds for a rodeo. But the traffic was horrendous.

The fact that he had been drinking didn't help matters. Earlier that day he had polished off a fifth of rum. Now, as he crept along in this giant traffic jam, the alcohol only increased his hostility. What really ticked him off were the cars that kept passing him on the right shoulder. Illegally. Again and again. Morgan shouted at the drivers. He shook his fist at them.

Then he looked in his rearview mirror. A Datsun was making a break for the shoulder of the road. Albert Morgan had had it. He pulled his loaded .22 caliber revolver from the glove compartment, reached past his wife and fired once through the open window of his Ford pickup truck.

Once was all it took.

The bullet—smaller than your fingernail—struck Paul Nussbaum just below the ear. Nussbaum, who had been a marathon runner and captain of his college tennis team, was paralyzed from the neck down.

It was the first of a rash of freeway shootings that summer. Morgan went to prison, convicted of attempted voluntary manslaughter. Nussbaum went into rehabilitation and a lifetime of pain.[1]

Hostility. Acts of violence seem to increasingly fill our newspapers. From freeway shootings to children throwing other children out of high-rise windows, it seems violence is becoming more and more random and rampant.

Hostility is like acid; it eats away at its container often extensively damaging it. In the mid 1950s, medical researchers first identified what came to be called "Type A" behavior. That was the term Dr. Meyer Friedman and Dr. Ray Rosenman used to describe a person who is always in a hurry and impatient, often hostile and angry. In contrast, "Type B" people are laid-back, calm, slow to anger, and good listeners. The doctors discovered "Type A's" had more heart attacks.

After thirty-five years of additional research, evidence clearly shows that the most harmful ingredient in this lethal mix is "free-floating hostility": being angry or on the point of anger much of the time, with or without cause.

Dr. Redford Williams, professor of psychiatry at the Duke University Medical Center in Durham, North Carolina, pinpoints the destructive nature of hatred. He estimates that about 20 percent of Americans have hostility levels high enough to endanger their health.[2]

Too often in Christian circles, anger is considered an emotion to be avoided at all costs. Some have even taught that it's a sin. But the Bible doesn't say that. Rather, God's Word admonishes us, "'In your anger do not sin': Do not let the sun go down while you are still angry, and do not give the devil a foothold" (Ephesians 4:26, 27).

Just what is anger, and what is the difference between it and hostility? Anger is an emotion, "a strong feeling of displeasure and usually of antagonism" according to Webster. In and of itself it is neither right nor wrong. But because it is so volatile, it can easily get sidetracked into destructive behavior.

Hostility, on the other hand, is anger that wants to hurt or punish. Often hostility is expressed in violence, either verbal or physical. This mishandling of anger is the real problem. Hostility is, in fact, a health hazard:

✔ Physically, hostility spurs the release of the hormone epinephrine (also called adrenaline), which makes the heart beat faster, leading to high blood pressure and increased risk of heart disease.

✔ Psychologically, hostile people have more conflicts and feel less satisfied with life. As Dr. Williams expresses it, "As a group, hostile people are unhappy."

✔ Socially, hostile people tend to be isolated (after all, who can stand to be with them?)

The case of the hostile prophet

In the Old Testament we meet an angry prophet. From him we can discover some principles to help us deal with this potentially deadly emotion.

By the time we meet Jonah in chapter four of the book of Jonah, he's registering an eight on the anger-hostility Richter scale. Remember the story? God has asked him to preach to the Assyrians, east in Nineveh. And so Jonah goes west, spiritually AWOL. Boarding a boat headed for Tarshish (probably Spain—as far west as Phoenician sailors went in 760 B.C.); he runs from God and ministry. But the Lord pursues Jonah with the power of nature. A frightening storm and three days in the belly of a giant fish finally convince Jonah that he had better obey the Lord.

So he comes to Nineveh and preaches: "On the first day Jonah started into the city. He proclaimed: 'Forty more days and Nineveh will be overturned" (Jonah 3:4). And the people respond! They believe the message, are shattered by the prophecy, and overwhelmed by God's kindness and mercy. They fast in repentance, and God forgives them: "When God saw what they did and how they turned from their evil ways, he had compassion and did not bring upon them the destruction he had threatened" (Jonah 3:10).

Jonah's body was pressured into going, but his heart was not converted. It is filled with anger, hate—and hostility. His feelings come pouring out in two angry outbursts.

Angry outburst number one:

> But Jonah was greatly displeased and became angry. He
> prayed to the Lord, "O Lord, is this not what I said when I was
> still at home? That is why I was so quick to flee to Tarshish. I
> knew that you are a gracious and compassionate God, slow to
> anger and abounding in love, a God who relents from sending
> calamity. Now, O Lord, take away my life for it is better for me
> to die than to live."
>
> But the Lord replied, "Have you any right to be angry?"
>
> Jonah 4:1-4

According to Dr. Williams in his book, *Anger Kills,* hostility
progresses through three stages:

Stage 1: Anger begins with an attitude of cynicism and dis-
trust. Suppose you are in the "nine items or less" line at the
grocery store. What does a person with a cynical, mistrusting
heart do? He starts counting the items in the baskets ahead of
him, of course! You expect someone to try to "cheat" you!

Stage 2: A feeling of anger comes over you. "I knew it! The
guy ahead of me has eleven items!"

Stage 3: Then comes the behavior of aggression and hostility.
You make a nasty remark to the "cheater."[3]

We see this progression in Jonah's attitude and behavior.
He's mad at the Assyrians and God! His mistrust and cynicism
are evident in verses one through three. He knew it! He just
knew if he went to Nineveh God might be merciful and spare
those sinners. The *New International Version's* rendering that he
is "greatly displeased" doesn't really do justice to the original
language. More literally it could be translated, "It was evil to
Jonah, a great evil calamity."

Then comes that feeling of anger and the behavior of aggression. He is so mad that he talks back to God! "I knew it! I knew
You'd forgive them!" In his criticism of God's love and mercy,
he seems to forget that he's recently received it in the belly of
the fish (Jonah 2:7, 8).

In his outburst we see one common characteristic of the hostile person. Hostile people tend to focus on self. Nine times in verses two and three Jonah uses the words "I" and "my." Hostility pushes out our concern for others and makes us self-absorbed.

Angry outburst number two:

> Jonah went out and sat down at a place east of the city. There he made himself a shelter, sat in its shade and waited to see what would happen to the city. Then the Lord God provided a vine and made it grow up over Jonah to give shade for his head to ease his discomfort, and Jonah was very happy about the vine. But at dawn the next day God provided a worm, which chewed the vine so that it withered. When the sun rose, God provided a scorching east wind, and the sun blazed on Jonah's head so that he grew faint. He wanted to die, and said, "it would be better for me to die than to live."
>
> But God said to Jonah, "Do you have a right to be angry about the vine?"
>
> "I do," he said. "I am angry enough to die."
>
> Jonah 4:5-9

A second characteristic of hostile anger is a loss of perspective.

When we are enraged, we lose sight of what is important. Like Albert Morgan, we believe and act as if it were worse to drive on the shoulder of the freeway than to shoot a human being. Jonah has lost all perspective. At first, he is angry because Nineveh isn't destroyed. Now he's angry because a plant is destroyed! He could care less about thousands of souls—but lose his shade? He goes "out of his gourd" with anger! So he sits there, pouting and whining to the Lord. He prefers plants over people.

Hostile people tend to be petty people. They live on the edge of rage. Little things send their blood pressure skyrocketing.

What ticks you off? Traffic is a common trigger in our society. A hostile person screams and swears at other drivers, even when the window is rolled up! Lazy, incompetent service pushes other people's buttons.

Hope for hostile hearts

What can we do about this destroyer of happiness?

The good news is that there is hope for hostile hearts.

As we saw in the chapter on resentment, there are four common ways to handle anger:

1. We can repress it (that is, force it down into the subconscious mind). The danger, though, is that a repressed hostility can cause severe depression.

2. We can suppress it (that is, consciously hold the anger in).

3. We can express it. Expressing hostility presents the kinds of problems we have examined so far. There was a time when some therapists encouraged people to express their anger in such faddish ways as Primal Scream Therapy. But that has fallen out of favor. In his book, *Anchors in Troubled Waters,* Batsell Barrett Baxter quotes well-known psychologist Dr. Leonard Berkowitz:

> Experimental psychologists, by and large, are skeptical of the energy theory that underlies ventilation therapies . . . depending upon the circumstances, a person's inhibitions might be lowered or his aggressive behavior might be reinforced, increasing the chances that the person will act aggressively outside the therapy situation . . . I do not think it is necessary to act out one's hostility.... We can talk about our feelings and describe our emotional reactions without attacking others verbally or physically, directly or in fantasy.[4]

4. We can confess it and deal with anger in a healthier way. While anger is not a sin, it needs safeguards to keep it from exploding. Let me suggest a few areas to work on:

✔ Improve your relationship with the Lord. Before Paul addresses the subject of anger in Ephesians 4, he looks first at our position in Christ:

> You were taught, with regard to your former way of life, to put off your old self, which is being corrupted by its deceitful desires; to be made new in the attitude of your minds; and to put on the new self, created to be like God in true righteousness and holiness.
>
> Ephesians 4:22-24

The beginning place for dealing with anger (or any other issue discussed in this book) is with the new birth. The Christian then needs to continue growing in Christ, and handling hostility and anger is an area to yield to Christ's control. Don't allow the "old nature" to rule. Let the Lord give you a new power for living and new perspectives on life.

Jonah had fallen back into old modes of thinking. He thought his happiness depended on the changing circumstances and conditions of life (like vines and winds) rather than the unchanging Creator/God. He was delighting more in God's blessings than in God.

✔ Deal with your anger honestly and quickly. Failure to do so leaves a wide-open door for Satan. But how can we deal with it quickly?

One way is to "reason with yourself."

Another way, as in Jonah's case, allow God to reason with you. Notice how God ministers to his angry prophet:

> But the Lord replied, "Have you any right to be angry?"
>
> . . .
>
> But God said to Jonah, "Do you have a right to be angry about the vine?"
>
> "I do," he said. "I am angry enough to die."
>
> But the Lord said, "You have been concerned about this vine, though you did not tend it or make it grow. It sprang up overnight and died overnight. But Nineveh has more than a

hundred and twenty thousand people who cannot tell their right
hand from their left, and many cattle as well. Should I not be
concerned about that great city?"   Jonah 4:4, 9-11

In effect, the Lord tells Jonah, "Listen to yourself . . . analyze
why you are so angry. Do you really have a right to feel this way?
Don't you see how out of proportion you have this whole thing?
Jonah, which is more important, people or plants? And if people
aren't important to you, how about their cows?"

In *Anger Kills,* Dr. Williams lists over a dozen strategies for
dealing with hostility. But the first one he lists is the one God
uses with Jonah, "Reason with yourself." Cut off the physical
feelings of hostility before they begin. Develop a better sense of
perspective. If God is merciful to us when we don't deserve it,
why not extend His mercy to others, even if they don't deserve
it? Why not be more patient with that incompetent clerk? That
inconsiderate driver?

Reason with yourself, and start developing patience (it is,
after all, a fruit of the Spirit). Dr. Williams reminds us of two
simple rules to live by:

* Don't sweat the small stuff.
* Most matters are small stuff.

As Proverbs 19:11 reminds us, "A man's wisdom gives him
patience; it is to his glory to overlook an offense."

Deal with hostility by redefining or deflecting the offense.

✔ Finally, improve your relationship with others. Learn to
listen more. Listening will help you be less focused on self.
Practice extending God's forgiveness to others. "Be kind and
compassionate to one another, forgiving each other, just as in
Christ God forgave you" (Ephesians 4:32).

There's hope for hostile hearts. We don't have to live on the
edge of rage, being a pain to others and harmful to our own
health. We can see that's true because of what happened to
Jonah. What did become of him? Did he remain angry and hostile? I think he "got the message." After all, that's why he wrote

this book, the most beautiful message of God's love for all people to be found in the Old Testament.

There's hope. You don't have to live your life like Ty Cobb, the well-known baseball player from the early part of this century. Cobb was a seething mass of hostility. He was cruel and nasty. He spiked opponents, brawled with teammates, and attacked men and women at any perceived slight.

He once bragged to his biographer that he beat a would-be mugger to death in 1912: "Left him there, not breathing, in his own rotten blood. I played the next day and got three base hits." That same year he stormed into the stands in New York to punch and kick a heckler. The man he attacked had no hands.

The mistrust and cynicism of the hostile personality are evident in Cobb's words, "I had to fight all my life to survive. They were all against me . . . tried every dirty trick to cut me down. But I beat the bastards and left them in the ditch." Cobb died in 1961. Alone.[5]

Life doesn't have to be lived that way. Shouldn't be lived that way.

Take your cue from Jonah, not Albert Morgan or Ty Cobb. In Christ, there's hope for hostile hearts.

66Winter, spring, summer or fall,
all you have to do is call.**99**

Carole King
You've Got a Friend

66A friend loves at all times,
and a brother is born for adversity.**99**

Proverbs 17:17

Chapter Seven

The Struggle for Self-Esteem

He began life with a lot of disadvantages.

His mother, who worked long, hard hours, was very domi-neering. In the course of her life she had run through three marriages. (The rumor was that her second husband left her be-cause she beat him regularly.) He received no love, discipline, or affection from his mother—in fact, she wouldn't even let him call her at work.

At school, he had few friends. He was lonely, ugly, poor, and rejected. So he dropped out of high school and joined the marines—maybe they could make a "man" of him. Unfortunately, all he found in the marines was more ridicule. So he responded in the only way he knew—he fought. All he received for his efforts was a dishonorable discharge.

As an adult, he still was unimpressive. Short and scrawny with a squeaky voice, he had no marketable skills. About the only thing he could do was accurately shoot a rifle. (The marines had taught him that much.) On a scale of one to ten, his self-worth was at minus three.

He thought a change of scenery might help, so he moved for a while to a foreign country. He married there and later moved back to the United States. But his marriage was soon in a sham-bles. His wife held him in contempt and bullied him. As punishment, she once locked him in the bathroom! He was unwanted and unloved. There wasn't an ounce of self-esteem in his body.

So on November 22, 1963, he took a rifle to his new job at a book storage building in Dallas. Later that day, Lee Harvey Oswald put two bullets into the back of President John F. Kennedy's head. JFK—handsome, wealthy, successful—with all the strengths and advantages that Oswald had never had.[1]

While the degree of violence in Oswald's story is unusual, the story is far too common. Too many children grow up feeling unloved and inferior, bitter about themselves in a world that worships rock stars and sports heroes.

Both Christian and non-Christian psychologists rank self-esteem as one of the basic human needs. In his book, *Reality Therapy,* William Glasser writes:

> Equal to the importance to the need for love is the need to
> feel that we are worthwhile both to ourselves and to others. . . .
> If we do not fulfill our need to feel worthwhile, we will suffer as
> acutely as when we fail to love or be loved.[2]

Many public and private schools have now made the same "discovery." Schools in Orange County, California, for instance, have participated in a parent-led program called "Project Self-Esteem" designed to develop greater self-esteem in children. It seems that kids who like themselves do well in school, while those with low self-esteem do poorly, both academically and relationally.

What is self-esteem? Is it really important? Is it biblical?

Some Christians recoil from terms such as "positive self-image," "self-esteem," and "self-love" equating them with pride and conceit. They mistakenly believe that humility and self-denial call for self-hatred. What, exactly, is self-esteem?

Simply put, it is the way we feel about ourselves. It is our personal judgment concerning ourselves.

Jesus tells us to love ourselves, as well as others:

> "Love the Lord your God with all your heart and with all your
> soul and with all your mind and with all your strength." The

second is this: "Love your neighbor as yourself." There is no
commandment greater than these.　　　　　Mark 12:30, 31

It would seem some form of self-love is appropriate and
necessary.

An epidemic of inferiority

As human beings made in God's image, we have the ability
to think about ourselves. We constantly engage in self-reflection.
We constantly evaluate ourselves, rating and ranking ourselves
on a scale based on the values and beliefs we've been taught
and we've internalized.

Today there is an epidemic of inferiority in our society, partly
because we have been using unbiblical measuring sticks on ourselves and each other. What are these wrong yardsticks of
self-worth? They boil down to four:

Beauty. Through the media, our society sets standards of
appearance few can meet.

Brawn. Many of the heroes of today, especially with young
people, are those who excel in physical and athletic ability.

Brains. If you haven't got either of the first two, you had better hope for a high IQ.

Bucks. Finally, if you have none of the above, your only
chance is to have money so you can purchase the "image" that
tells others you've got it all together.

But most of us can relate better to "Peanuts'" Charlie Brown
than to Michael Jordan or Julia Roberts. Poor Charlie Brown!
He's funny-looking and only an average student. He pitches his
heart out, but his baseball team never wins. He's a walking disaster. One comic strip pictured him moaning to Linus, "Nobody
appreciates how wishy-washy people suffer. Our lives are in constant torment. You know what wishy-washy people need? Cringe
benefits!"

When a society measures people by how they look or how
they perform, the poor Charlie Browns are always being put

down and humiliated. As George Gobel once lamented, "Did you ever get the feeling that the world is a tuxedo and you are a pair of brown shoes?"

But God defines us first and foremost by who we are—flawed and sinful, yes, but beautiful creatures made in His image. Men and women, children and teens for whom Christ died. If we are ever to fully appreciate our worth in God's eyes, we've got to stop looking at ourselves through the tinted glasses of Madison Avenue.

Some have compared low self-esteem to a cancer. It eats away at all aspects of our lives and relationships. It increases loneliness and isolation; it breeds depression, anger, and criticism; it makes it hard to build friendships and other relationships; it can even affect our physical health and bring on digestive problems and high blood pressure.

In the Old Testament, we meet a man who went from the heights of conceit to the depths of self-deprecation. In his discovery of the proper balance, we can learn some keys to healthy and biblical self-esteem.

From palace to plains

Moses is born at a difficult time in Israel's history. Enslaved in Egypt, the Israelites are under Pharaoh's edict that calls for the death of all male babies. But through the sovereignty of God, Moses is rescued from the Nile by Pharaoh's own daughter and is raised in Pharaoh's household. God has delivered him to be a deliverer.

The day finally comes when he chooses to identify with his people, the Israelites:

> One day, after Moses had grown up, he went out to where his own people were and watched them at their hard labor. He saw an Egyptian beating a Hebrew, one of his own people. Glancing this way and that and seeing no one, he killed the Egyptian and hid him in the sand.   Exodus 2:11, 12

Moses tries to deliver the people his way, not God's. Perhaps conceit and pride are involved. As many passages of Scripture point out, pride is indeed a sin.

Pride and conceit are never pretty. The story is told of two actresses who were talking backstage at the final curtain of their play. "What's wrong with the leading lady?" asked one, "She's acting very angry."

"She received only nine bouquets over the footlights," replied the other.

"Nine? Isn't that pretty good?"

"Yes, but she paid for ten!"

That's pride at work. Exaggerating and magnifying our talents. Bragging and overvaluing ourselves. Ignoring and concealing our shortcomings. But pride isn't the same as self-esteem.

Note Proverbs 27:2:

> Let another praise you, and not your own mouth;
> someone else, and not your own lips.

It's OK to be praised. That's not sinful. But don't brag on and praise yourself. Unfortunately, too many people (including Christians) cannot graciously accept praise from others. But it's really OK to feel good about yourself and to accept the plaudits of others (reread Proverbs 27:2).

Perhaps, in this early incident, Moses is having a problem with pride and conceit. Maybe he just has unrealistic expectations of himself, and who he is falls short of who he thinks he should be. Whatever the case, when we meet him next he's a different man.

Forty years have passed when one day Moses walks over to check out an unusual sight—a bush that blazes but doesn't burn up. The Moses we meet at this point is no longer the brash, young deliverer we saw earlier. He's a discouraged, aging, nobody in a dead-end shepherding job in the middle of nowhere. His problem is no longer pride—it's now an extreme case of low self-esteem.

Three keys to self-esteem

In his book, *Feeling Free,* Archibald Hart lists three steps towards developing a healthy self-image:

1. The acceptance of God's unconditional love
2. The development of realistic self-knowledge
3. Complete self-acceptance[3]

In Moses' journey to a healthy self-image, we see these three keys at work.

> When the Lord saw that he had gone over to look, God
> called to him from within the bush, "Moses! Moses!"
> And Moses said, "Here I am."   Exodus 3:4

God calls Moses by name. There are no put-downs or reprimands. And that's what Moses needs most—to discover and accept God's unconditional love. That's the first key to true self-esteem.

Isn't God's grace amazing? He loves you and me just as we are. Who do we think we are not to love ourselves? You and I are unique, made in God's image (Genesis 1:25, 26).

God is the God of Moses' family (Exodus 3:6). He loves him and cares about him. And He has a task for him—to deliver the Israelites from Egypt.

Unfortunately, because low self-esteem develops over many years, it can become deeply ingrained and difficult to weed out. Moses has been in the wilderness for forty years. Undoubtedly, the memory of his failures has been running over and over again through his mind like an irritating tune you just can't forget.

It's often a long, slow process to reconstruct a demolished self-image. There are no instant cures. God wades patiently through all of Moses' excuses.

Excuse number one:

> But Moses said to God, "Who am I, that I should go to
> Pharaoh and bring the Israelites out of Egypt?"
>
>   Exodus 3:11

Translation: "I'm just a nobody. I'm not qualified. I can't do a big job like that." And, in essence, God agrees! But then He promises, "I will be with you" (Exodus 3:12).

Excuse number two:

> Moses said to God, "Suppose I go to the Israelites and say to them, 'The God of your fathers has sent me to you,' and they ask me, 'What is his name?' Then what shall I tell them?"
>
> Exodus 3:13

Translation: "Who are You, God? I'm a little—no, make that a lot—confused!"

Patiently, God reveals himself. "I am who I am." Then the Lord assures Moses that the Israelites really will listen (Exodus 3:14-22).

Excuse number three:

> Moses answered, "What if they do not believe me or listen to me and say, 'The Lord did not appear to you'?"
>
> Exodus 4:1

Translation: "Come on, Lord—they wouldn't believe a nobody like me!" To help Moses overcome this potential credibility gap, God gives him three signs to verify his message (Exodus 4:2-9).

Up to this point, God has been patiently helping Moses accept His love and help, and get to know Him better. But Moses' fourth excuse reveals his real problem—a combination of low self-esteem and a lack of faith.

Excuse number four:

> Moses said to the Lord, "O Lord, I have never been eloquent, neither in the past nor since you have spoken to your servant. I am slow of speech and tongue."
>
> Exodus 4:10

Translation: "Listen, Lord, I get tongue-tied in front of large groups. And I've talked only to my sheep and my family for the past forty years." Moses has messed up once, and now his sense of inferiority is causing him to exaggerate his weaknesses.

This brings us to the second key to self-esteem: We have to develop realistic self-knowledge. We must face honestly who and what we are.

It is at this point that pride differs from self-esteem. Pride is *unrealistic* self-knowledge. Pride exaggerates strengths in order to hide weaknesses. When we are proud, we are being dishonest with ourselves. Healthy self-esteem, on the other hand, faces up realistically both to our strengths and our weaknesses. It causes us to be transparently honest with ourselves. Moses has a distorted view of himself. He has blown his failings and shortcomings all out of proportion, while minimizing his strengths. So God begins to help him develop a realistic self-knowledge:

> The Lord said to him, "Who gave man his mouth? Who makes him deaf or mute? Who gives him sight or makes him blind? Is it not I, the Lord? Now go; I will help you speak and will teach you what to say."   Exodus 4:11, 12

Too many Christians, like Moses, exaggerate their weaknesses and come up with long lists of reasons for not serving God. They need to remember Paul's prescription for healthy self-esteem:

> For by the grace given me I say to every one of you: Do not think of yourself more highly than you ought, but rather think of yourself with sober judgment, in accordance with the measure of faith God has given you.   Romans 12:3

See how a healthy self-image lies between the extremes of pride and self-deprecation? We have to be honest with ourselves regarding our strengths and weaknesses. We have to appraise ourselves accurately.

Several years ago, before he set what was then a new indoor pole vault record, Billy Olson was asked if he might someday break the once unthinkable height of twenty feet. He replied, "I think it's inevitable that someone is going to get there. I see several guys in the world who are capable of jumping that high." The interviewer's evaluation was revealing: "Billy doesn't come right out and say he'll be the first to do it. But he doesn't say he won't either."[4]

That's a healthy, balanced self-esteem. No bragging or conceit, but no self-deprecating put-downs either. Just a matter-of-fact, honest self appraisal.

Poor Moses. He is feeling afraid and inadequate. He finally stops making excuses and just says no: "O Lord, please send someone else" (Exodus 4:13).

Translation: "Not me, Lord, I'm scared spitless!"

God finally gets angry with Moses' whining and promises him that his brother Aaron can be his mouthpiece. Then He sends him on his way (Exodus 4:14-17). But Moses is not yet cured of his low self-esteem.

The third key to self-esteem is reaching complete self-acceptance. We begin, as we saw, by accepting God's love for us; then we start being honest and realistic with ourselves; and finally, gradually, we come to accept ourselves. Eventually, even Moses reached this point. Watch the progression of speakers in the following passages.

Exodus 5:3: "Then they said . . ."

Exodus 7:1, 2: "Aaron is to tell Pharaoh. . ."

Exodus 8:9: "Moses said . . ."

Exodus 12:21: "Then Moses . . . said to them."

Each of us is a unique combination of strengths and weaknesses. By God's grace we have to start accepting our own unique mix, using the strengths we possess and accepting our weaknesses. Each of us must, as well, come to realize that, from God's perspective, the meek are leaders, the slaves are free, the last are first, and weakness is power.

> That is why, for Christ's sake, I delight in weaknesses, in
> insults, in hardships, in persecutions, in difficulties. For when I
> am weak, then I am strong.   2 Corinthians 12:10

As time passed, Moses grew more God-confident, his self-esteem became healthier, and he started doing what God had sent him to do.

We know something Moses didn't know, don't we? We know about the cross of Christ. Someone has said that the cross is "God's price tag on the human soul." We're of infinite worth—Christ died for us! Being a sinner doesn't mean we're worthless. God can forgive us and make us new.]

We're valuable—created in the image of God. We're of infinite worth—Christ died for each one of us. And true self-esteem is found only in Him.

Undoubtedly the most widely-known and best-loved prayer written in the twentieth century is Reinhold Niebuhr's "Serenity Prayer." The U.S.O. distributed millions of copies of it during World War II. Alcoholics Anonymous adopted it as an official motto. You may have a copy of it on a plaque or bookmark in your home. To discover and maintain a healthy, Biblical self esteem, we need to heed and apply these three truths. Why don't you quietly pray them right now:

God, grant me the serenity
to accept the things I cannot change,
the courage to change the things I can,
and wisdom to know the difference.

Chapter Eight

Building Lasting Friendships

It was in 1967 that Gale Sayers and Brian Piccolo, running backs for the Chicago Bears, began rooming together. This was both a professional and a personal first: a first in race relations for the professional football league, and a first for Sayers and Piccolo as well. Sayers, an African American, had never had a close association with a white before and Piccolo, a Caucasian, was in the same position in regard to blacks.

Over the next two football seasons, their friendship grew until their loyalty to one another was deeply cemented. *Brian's Song,* a movie based on their friendship, movingly demonstrates how their relationship became one of the best and deepest in sports history.

But in the middle of the 1969 season, Piccolo was diagnosed with cancer. He still wanted to play football, but he spent more time in hospital beds than behind the line of scrimmage. As often as he could, Sayers flew to be with him.

Gale Sayers was scheduled to receive the George S. Halas Award that year at the Professional Football Writers annual dinner in New York. He had been chosen as the most courageous player in pro football. Together with their wives, Sayers and Piccolo had planned to attend the dinner, but the cancer kept "Pick" confined to bed.

As he received the trophy, tears came to Sayers's eyes. The normally reticent Sayers said:

> You flatter me by giving me this award, but I tell you here
> and now that I accept it for Brian Piccolo. Brian Piccolo is the
> man of courage who should receive the George S. Halas Award. I
> love Brian Piccolo and I'd like you to love him. Tonight, when
> you hit your knees, please ask God to love him too.[1]

"I love Brian Piccolo." It's not very often that we hear words
like that from one man about another. In the past hundred
years, especially in the United States, that kind of
"friendship/love" has come to be the exception rather than the
rule, especially among men. Women seem to do a far better job
of making friends than men. When asked, "How many men
have real friendships?" psychologists and therapists usually es-
timate only about 10 percent We have co-workers, companions
and acquaintances—but that's not the same as the deep friend-
ship/love of a Gale Sayers and a Brian Piccolo.

More often than not we have "safe" relationships—a helping
hand, "convenience" friendship, a doing-things-together friendship, a sharing-past-memories friendship. Dr. Michael McGill, in
his report on male intimacy, painted it this way:

> Men have functional friendships. They may have tennis
> friends, business friends, neighborhood friends that they talk to
> about lawns and fertilizers. With none of those friends has he a
> context where he can talk about things emotional.[2]

As legitimate as all of those types of friendships are, it seems
that most men (and many women) consider anything else too
risky.

Why?

There are at least two major reasons:

(1) American men are programmed with the message, "Show
any weakness and we'll clobber you with it." We believe we
must always be self-reliant and strong.

A cartoon that appeared in *Leadership* magazine expressed it
well. It depicted a male usher greeting a visitor (another man) at

the church door: "Welcome to Lake Road Church, 'Where we love everybody' . . . in that macho, moose-killing way we men have, of course!"[3]

Dr. McGill, who is associated with Southern Methodist University, comments, "Men are not more loving and open because they want to retain power and mystery, and fear a show of feeling."[4]

(2) The other reason we men avoid deeper friendships is that we fear being considered homosexual. As a result we have allowed the increasingly strident agenda of the homosexual community to rob us of the beauty of true, deeply-felt friendships.

History, however, is replete with examples of strong male friendships. Most of us probably are familiar with these lines from the English poet, Alfred Lord Tennyson:

> 'Tis better to have loved and lost
> than never to have loved at all.

What most of us don't realize is that he wrote those words about a man, not a woman. The lines are from his poem, "In Memoriam," written as a tribute to his friend, Arthur Hallam, after Hallam's tragic death at age twenty-two. They were best friends, not lovers. Hallam had, in fact, been engaged to Tennyson's sister.

Going back further in western civilization, we find that Aristotle classed friendship/love among the virtues. The Greeks had a special word to describe it—philia (hence, the name Philadelphia—the "city of brotherly love"). The Greeks had a different word for sexual love—eros. In *The Four Loves*, C. S. Lewis summarizes our contemporary dilemma when he writes:

> On a broad historical view it is, of course, not the demonstrative gestures of friendship among our ancestors but the absence of such gestures in our own society that calls for some special explanation. We, not they, are out of step.[5]

In our cities and across our nation, loneliness is a raging epidemic. We need to rediscover how to build relationships—deep friendships—with others. Let's turn our attention to one of the most famous friendships of all history, and from that relationship discover four necessary factors in building solid, deep friendships.

How to build a friendship

The place: Israel.

The time: about 1020 B.C.

Saul may be the king, but there's a new star on the scene; David, the slayer of Goliath. And while the insecure king is beginning to worry about this young hero, Jonathan, his son and heir to the throne, is quite impressed.

> After David had finished talking with Saul, Jonathan became one in spirit with David, and he loved him as himself. From that day Saul kept David with him and did not let him return to his father's house. And Jonathan made a covenant with David because he loved him as himself. Jonathan took off the robe he was wearing and gave it to David, along with his tunic, and even his sword, his bow and his belt.   1 Samuel 18:1-4

Why is Jonathan so taken with David? For one thing, both are men after God's own heart, sharing a common faith in God's power and majesty.

David's faith had been demonstrated when he stood up to the giant. Jonathan's attitude was apparent when the Philistine army besieged Israel at Micmash. Jonathan, accompanied only by his armor bearer, staged a one-man surprise attack that led to a great victory because of his faith in God (1 Samuel 13:16—14:23).

Now, as Jonathan looks at David, he sees someone "who saw the same truth," as C. S. Lewis phrased it. Jonathan has found a real "soul brother."

This illuminates the first factor in building a friendship:

(1) The discovery of *mutual interests and a mutual faith*.

Their souls were "knit" together—literally, in the Hebrew, "chained" together. Their common courageous faith bridged the social chasm between the crown prince and the young shepherd.

Deep friendships usually start here, in companionship, then grow beyond.

(2) A second factor in a growing friendship is *mutual acceptance*.

Carl Rogers has said, "True friendships cannot be built until we destroy the idea of what the other person should be."[6]

It is up to Jonathan, as son of the king, to bridge the social gap. He takes the initiative in extending the covenant of friendship by honoring David through the giving of gifts as tokens of his friendship (his royal robe, armor, sword, bow, and belt). In effect, Jonathan is saying, "I accept you as you are."

One of the best ways we demonstrate our acceptance of others is to listen. Most of us would rather talk, but if you want to have friends, learn to listen! As someone put it, "The reason a dog has so many friends is that he wags his tail instead of his tongue."

Learn to accept and to listen to others.

(3) A third factor in building friendships is *mutual honesty*. Real friendships demand openness and transparency.

As Saul's paranoia concerning David deepened, Jonathan was honest enough to confront the evil in his father and to see the goodness in his friend:

> Saul told his son Jonathan and all the attendants to kill David. But Jonathan was very fond of David and warned him, "My father Saul is looking for a chance to kill you."
>
> . . . .
>
> Jonathan spoke well of David to Saul his father and said to him, "Let not the king do wrong to his servant David: he has not wronged you, and what he has done has benefited you greatly."

. . . .

> Saul listened to Jonathan and took this oath: "As surely as
> the Lord lives, David will not be put to death."
>
> 1 Samuel 19:1, 2, 4, 6

Jonathan is open and truthful with David. He goes to bat for him with his father and he is able to heal the breach—if only temporarily. It's sometimes hard to be honest and open with each other. But honesty promotes healthy friendships. When we have low self-esteem and fear rejection by others, we hide behind masks and build walls around ourselves. We're afraid to let others know what we're really like, fearful that they won't accept us. That's why healthy, biblical self-esteem is so important in building relationships.

God has called us to be authentic and real. We need to strive for open, honest relationships. Honesty doesn't mean being argumentative or hurting others through our words. Rather, it means "leveling" with each other in a sensitive, loving way. C. S. Lewis, drawing a distinction between sexual love and friendship, put it this way: "Eros will have naked bodies; friendship, naked personalities."[7]

(4) The fourth factor in building a strong friendship is *mutual loyalty.* And it is this factor of commitment and faithfulness that is so strikingly evident in the relationship of David and Jonathan.

Once again Saul attempts to kill David (1 Samuel 19:9, 10). David goes into hiding. Based on his father's previous promises, Jonathan doesn't want to believe that David's life is in danger:

> Then David fled from Naioth at Ramah and went to
> Jonathan, and asked, "What have I done? What is my crime?
> How have I wronged your father, that he is trying to take
> my life?"
>
> "Never!" Jonathan replied. "You are not going to die! Look,
> my father doesn't do anything, great or small, without confiding
> in me. Why would he hide this from me? It's not so!"

But David took an oath and said, "Your father knows very
well that I have found favor in your eyes, and he has said to himself, 'Jonathan must not know this or he will be grieved.' Yet as
surely as the Lord lives and as you live, there is only a step
between me and death."

Jonathan said to David, "Whatever you want me to do, I'll do
for you."   Samuel 20: 1-4

That's a loyal friend—one who asks, "What do you want me
to do?" Together, they concoct a scheme to test Saul:

Then Jonathan said to David: "By the Lord, the God of Israel,
I will surely sound out my father by this time the day after
tomorrow! If he is favorably disposed toward you, will I not send
you word and let you know? But if my father is inclined to harm
you, may the Lord deal with me, be it ever so severely, if I do not
let you know and send you away safely."   1 Samuel 20:12, 13

Then they renewed their covenant of friendship:

So Jonathan made a covenant with the house of David, saying, "May the Lord call David's enemies to account." And
Jonathan had David reaffirm his oath out of love for him,
because he loved him as he loved himself.   1 Samuel 20:16, 17

Jonathan's heart breaks when he discovers that, in fact, his
father is seeking to kill David. "He did not eat, because he was
grieved at his father's shameful treatment of David" (1 Samuel
20:34).

Commitment is vital, yet greatly undervalued in our society.
Loyalty and commitment are key ingredients in making a marriage last, they're important to the walk of discipleship, and
they're vital to building deep friendships.

Soon after Jack Benny died, George Burns was interviewed on
a television talk show. Asked about his friendship with Benny,
he flicked his ever-present cigar and said:

> Jack and I had a wonderful friendship for nearly fifty-five
> years. Jack never walked out on me when I sang a song and I
> never walked out on him when he played the violin. We laughed
> together, we played together, we worked together, we ate
> together. I suppose that for many of those years we talked every
> single day.[8]

Mutual loyalty! That was the kind of friendship/commitment
that Burns and Benny had for each other, and that was the kind
of loyalty that Jonathan had for David.

As King Saul's hostility grows, Jonathan refuses to turn on his
friend, even at the risk of losing the throne. Adversity truly
proves his friendship: "A friend loves at all times, and a brother
is born for adversity" (Proverbs 17:17).

Warning David by a prearranged sign (1 Samuel 20:35-40),
Jonathan meets with his friend one last time.

> David got up from the south side of the stone, and bowed down
> before Jonathan three times, with his face to the ground. Then
> they kissed each other and wept together—but David wept the
> most.
> Jonathan said to David, "Go in peace, for we have sworn
> friendship with each other in the name of the Lord, saying, 'The
> Lord is witness between you and me, and between your descen-
> dants and descendants forever.'" Then David left, and Jonathan
> went back to the town.   1 Samuel 20:41, 42

Some have tried to justify homosexual behavior by claiming
that David and Jonathan were lovers. Although that might be
"politically correct" in some quarters, it is not biblically correct!
They were not homosexuals—they were best friends. As
Frederick Buechner wrote in his book, *Peculiar Treasures:*

> . . . both emotions and the language used to express them
> ran a good deal higher in the ancient Near East than they do in

Little Rock, Arkansas, or Boston, Massachusetts, or even Los
Angeles, California, and for that and other reasons the theory
that such passages as have been cited necessarily indicate a
homosexual relationship is almost certainly false. . . . it's sad,
putting it mildly, that we live at a time when in many quarters
two men can't embrace or weep together or speak of loving one
another without arousing the suspicion that they must also go to
bed together.[9]

Their friendship/love is epitomized in David's lament upon
learning of Jonathan's death in battle:

> "How the mighty have fallen in battle!
> 　　Jonathan lies slain on your heights.
> I grieve for you, Jonathan my brother;
> 　　you were very dear to me.
> Your love for me was wonderful,
> 　　more wonderful than that of women.
> "How the mighty have fallen!
> 　　The weapons of war have perished!"
>
> 2 Samuel 1:25-27

Philia—friendship love—is a beautiful thing. Let's not rob
genuine friendship of its power, loyalty, and goodness.

In my own life, it was just a few short years ago that I finally
discovered the real beauty of friendship. As an only child and an
American male, I faced a number of barriers in this area. But the
Lord broke down the wall of fear I had concerning self-revela-
tions, and I discovered a male friend with whom I can talk
about deeper things than sports or the weather; a friend with
whom I can share mutual interests, such as music, and a mutual
faith in God; a friend who accepts me as I am, knowing my failings; a friend who is honest with me and loyal to my best
interests. And I try to respond to him in the same way. Finding
that philia (friendship/love) was a new experience for me, and
one that I treasure to this day.

A closing thought

It was said that Al Jolson (actor, vaudeville entertainer, and the first person to star in a "talking picture") was a difficult man to deal with in making a picture. The story is told of a young director who, in rehearsal, once tried to persuade him to change part of a scene. The director soon found himself in trouble!

Jolson stopped the action, turned on the young man and said scornfully, "Listen, kid, I've got a million dollars. What do you have?"

"Friends," said the director quietly.

The writer Robert Louis Stevenson once said, "A friend is a present you give yourself."

Let me encourage you to give yourself a friend—and soon!

Chapter Nine

The Perils of Peers

Len Bias was a six-foot, eight-inch All-American basketball player for the University of Maryland. By the close of his senior year he was the highest scorer in the school's history.

But being a college scoring leader wasn't his wildest dream. He wanted to play for the Boston Celtics. He pursued that dream with a religious fervor, getting to know Red Auerbach, the Celtics' president and asking to be drafted.

The dream came true on a Tuesday in June of 1986 when the Celtics named Len as their first NBA draft pick.

The next hours were frantic and exhausting. Bias flew to Boston for interviews and to thank Auerbach for choosing him. On Wednesday, the newest NBA star signed a ten-year, multi-million-dollar endorsement deal with Reebok shoes. After a reception that evening, he flew back to Maryland.

By Thursday morning, Len Bias was dead.

The cause of death listed on the death certificate was "cocaine intoxication." But the actual cause was a "friend" who, late Wednesday night, took Bias into a Washington, DC neighborhood known as an easy place to find drugs. Len Bias "celebrated"—for the first, and the last time.[1]

The deaths of two young athletes that summer of 1986, Len Bias and the Cleveland Brown's free safety, Don Rogers, helped fuel the "Just Say No" anti-drug campaign of the late 1980s.

Perhaps a more effective campaign would have been to teach and train people in the art of choosing friends.

Friends are important. We weren't created to live alone, but were made, rather, as social creatures who need one another. The Bible recognizes the value of relationships and places a high premium on friendship:

> A friend loves at all times, and a brother is born for adversity.
>
> Proverbs 17:17

But Scripture also warns us of the dangers of some types of "friends" and of the necessity of choosing our friends carefully:

> My son, if sinners entice you,
>   do not give in to them.
> If they say, "Come along with us;
>   let's lie in wait for someone's blood,
>   let's waylay some harmless soul;
>
>   . . . .
>
> we will get all sorts of valuable things
>   and fill our house with plunder;
> throw in your lot with us,
>   and we will share a common purse"—
> my son, do not go along with them,
>   do not set foot on their paths;
>
>   . . . .
>
> These men lie in wait for their own blood;
>   they waylay only themselves!
> Such is the end of all who go after ill-gotten gain;
>   it takes away the lives of those who get it.
>
> Proverbs 1:10, 11, 13-15, 18, 19

But the perils of peer pressure are not just a reality for teenagers and young adults like Len Bias. For good or ill, the peer pressure of our friends, companions, and associates influences all of us. A youth minister I know wrote the following article for his church bulletin:

"Who said that tan pants and navy blue sport coats look
good?" This statement was made by one of the teens here . . . in
response to seeing so many people dressed in this fashion that it
appeared to be some sort of uniform. Now this doesn't mean
that tan pants and navy jackets are bad, but it does indicate that
we may be affected by peer pressure more than we care to admit.
Nobody is exempt from the pressures of our peers, whether
teenage or adult.

"Amnon had a friend"

In the Old Testament, we meet a young man who is rich and
powerful. He is, in fact, the crown prince of Israel. But his fool-
ish selection of a friend, and his acquiescing to the friend's
advice proves to be his undoing.

Amnon is David's oldest son by his wife Ahinoam of Jezreel
(2 Samuel 3:2). As time passes, Amnon develops a "crush" on
his half-sister, Tamar. (She and her brother Absalom are David's
children by one of his other wives, Maacah).

> In the course of time, Amnon son of David fell in love with
> Tamar, the beautiful sister of Absalom son of David.
>
> 2 Samuel 13:1

Unfortunately, Amnon follows his father's example. King
David's lack of self-control in taking Bathsheba and murdering
her husband demonstrated an abuse of power that wasn't lost
on his children. The prophet Nathan had sounded God' omi-
nous warning:

> "Now, therefore, the sword will never depart from your house,
> because you despised me and took the wife of Uriah the Hittite
> to be your own."   2 Samuel 12:10

Now this prophecy slowly unfolds as Amnon allows his
desires and passions to enslave him:

> Amnon became frustrated to the point of illness on account
> of his sister Tamar, for she was a virgin, and it seemed impossi-
> ble for him to do anything to her.
>
> 2 Samuel 13:2

He is so overwhelmed by his lusts that he makes himself sick!

Today's world encourages us to be "open minded and objective." But believers must reaffirm the truth that there can be no compromise with sin and evil, even in the area of our thoughts. Scripture advises us to be careful of our thought life:

> Above all else, guard your heart, for it is the wellspring of life.
>
> Proverbs 4:23

Rather than entertaining evil thoughts, we must "hate what is evil and cling to what is good" (Romans 12:9). We can't play with sin, dwell on it, and allow it to take root in our hearts and minds, then expect it not to grow. Sin is an awful taskmaster— as Amnon will discover. He fails to control his sexual fantasies and the results are devastating.

> Now Amnon had a friend named Jonadab son of Shimeah,
> David's brother. Jonadab was a very shrewd man. He asked
> Amnon, "Why do you, the king's son, look so haggard morning,
> after morning? Won't you tell me?"
>
> Amnon said to him, "I'm in love with Tamar, my brother
> Absalom's sister."
>
> "Go to bed and pretend to be ill," Jonadab said, "When your
> father comes to see you, say to him, 'I would like my sister
> Tamar to come and give me something to eat. Let her prepare
> the food in my sight so I may watch her and then eat it from her
> hand.'"
>
> 2 Samuel 13:3-5

"Amnon had a friend . . ." Those words should point to support and companionship. If Jonadab is a true friend, he should encourage the best in and for Amnon. But that is not the case. Amnon's "friend" leads him into sin.

It is vital that adults, as well as teens, choose their friends carefully. As the apostle Paul reminds us, "Bad company corrupts good character" (1 Corinthians 15:33). We all contend with peer pressure, though it seems especially troublesome for teens and young adults. The writer, Pearl Buck, once observed:

> Youth is the age of temptation and the greatest temptation of all is to do what the rest of the gang are doing, right or wrong. Too often it is wrong, for wisdom comes only with maturity, and the road to maturity of self-understanding and self-discipline is long and hard and there are those who never reach the end of the road.[2]

The "well-meaning" advice of our friends can encourage us to do good, or it can push us over the brink into evil.

How many Christians have sat over coffee with a friend who said, "You shouldn't have to take that! Why don't you divorce him," rather than, "Let's pray about this situation and how the Lord can strengthen your marriage."

How many college students have been told, "Go ahead and cheat—everybody does it," instead of, "Let's study together and see if we can ace this exam."

Too often we're like Dennis the Menace who lamented to his mother, "My conscience told me not to do it, but I decided to go along with Tommy's conscience instead."

Unfortunately for Amnon, he, too, takes his friend's advice. He pretends to be ill and asks his father, David, to have Tamar take care of him. When she brings him a loaf of freshly baked bread, he grabs her. With her arm in his vice-like grip, he blurts out what's really on his mind: "Come to bed with me, my sister."

Shaking with fear, Tamar attempts to reason with him: "Don't, my brother! Don't force me. Such a thing should not be done in Israel! Don't do this wicked thing. What about me? Where could I get rid of my disgrace? And what about you? You would be like one of the wicked fools in Israel. Please speak to the king; he will not keep me from being married to you."

But Amnon is beyond caring about her or even his own future. He refuses to listen to her words—and rapes her.

With his fantasies and lusts satisfied, Amnon's "love" quickly transforms itself into a deep hatred. "Get up and get out!" he snarls. In spite of her heart-rending pleas, Amnon has Tamar thrown out of his room (2 Samuel 13:11-18).

She is, not surprisingly, devastated by the rape:

> Tamar put ashes on her head and tore the ornamented robe she was wearing. She put her hand on her head and went away, weeping aloud as she went.   2 Samuel 13:19

Like a 7.2 earthquake, the shock waves reverberate through the palace household. King David is furious, yet he does nothing. Perhaps David is still weighed down with guilt for his own sin and the bad example he has set for his son. Perhaps he blames himself, feeling he's never been much of a father, always off on wars and kingdom business. Maybe he just doesn't know what to do. For whatever reason, David does nothing, and his failure to act decisively only makes the situation worse. A far greater tragedy is inevitable.

Tamar's life is not the only one ruined by Amnon's act. Her brother Absalom's life is disabled as well. Awkwardly, he attempts to comfort her, as he invites her to live at his house: "Has that Amnon, your brother, been with you? Be quiet now, my sister; he is your brother. Don't take this thing to heart" (2 Samuel 13:20).

But it is Absalom who takes it to heart. As he broods over the wrong that has been done to his sister, he is eaten up with resentment and bitterness:

> Absalom never said a word to Amnon, either good or bad; he hated Amnon because he had disgraced his sister Tamar.
>   2 Samuel 13:22

Absalom hides his hatred for two long years. Then, at last he gets his chance for vengeance. His shepherds are having a "sheep-shearing party," a festive occasion in that day and time. Absalom invites all his brothers to attend the party, then he waits for just the right moment. It isn't long in coming:

> Absalom ordered his men, "Listen! When Amnon is in high spirits from drinking wine and I say to you, 'Strike Amnon down,' then kill him. Don't be afraid. Have not I given you this order? Be strong and brave." So Absalom's men did to Amnon what Absalom had ordered. Then all the king's sons got up, mounted their mules and fled. 2 Samuel 13:28, 29

The first news dispatch back to the Jerusalem palace reports that all of the king's sons have been slain by Absalom and his men. Overcome by grief, King David goes into mourning (2 Samuel 13:30, 31).

But notice who brings David the correct facts regarding Amnon's death:

> But Jonadab son of Shimeah, David's brother, said, "My lord should not think that they killed all the princes; only Amnon is dead. This has been Absalom's expressed intention ever since the day Amnon raped his sister Tamar. My lord the king should not be concerned about the report that all the king's sons are dead. Only Amnon is dead." 2 Samuel 13:32, 33

When the smoke clears and the blood dries, only "Mr. Cool," Amnon's so-called friend, Jonadab, is left standing unscathed. Isn't that how it usually works? When someone gives us rotten advise and we follow it, we're the ones who pay the high price for sin—not him.

"I was helping Jim."

In 1987, the religious world was rocked by charges of sexual misconduct against Jim Bakker, founder of the PTL (Praise the Lord) ministries. As the story unfolded, it became clear that he was, indeed, guilty, not only of the original charge, but of many other misdeeds, both sexual and financial.

But it was the rape allegation raised by Jessica Hahn that started the avalanche. And, as Charles Shepard carefully documents in *Forgiven: The Rise and Fall of Jim Bakker and the PTL,* that incident involved the tie-in of—a "friend."

John Wesley Fletcher had joined the PTL ministries in 1979. Originally a traveling faith healer, he became a regular on the PTL broadcasts in 1980. As the months went by, he and Bakker became close friends. As Jim and Tammy's marriage slowly unraveled, Fletcher became a convenient shoulder to cry on.

On a Saturday in December, 1980, Bakker was at the Sheraton Inn in Clearwater, Florida, for a fund-raising telethon. Fletcher flew in a friend from New York, twenty-one-year-old Jessica Hahn. He later claimed he did it as a favor for Bakker. He was trying to "help" Bakker by making Tammy jealous, he said. As the sex scandal was about to break seven years later (along with the story of the $265,000 hush money) Fletcher told a reporter, "I did it because I honest to God believed I was helping Jim. I had no other motive."[3]

None of us needs that kind of "help." None of us needs a "friend" like that.

Perhaps John Wesley Fletcher's brand of friendship is best revealed at the end of the scandal. As Jim Bakker went off to the federal penitentiary, Fletcher, like Jonadab, stayed safely behind telling, and selling, his story to *Penthouse* magazine.

Real friends—godly friends—want the best for you. Even when it hurts: "Wounds from a friend can be trusted, but an enemy multiplies kisses" (Proverbs 27:6).

Fair-weather friends who "multiply kisses" always look out for number one. Their motto is, "A friend in need is no friend of mine!"

Amnon discovered the lies too late. Promising to free us from restrictions, sin enslaves us to our passions. Promising happiness, it bring heartbreak. Promising a full life, it delivers only death. Amnon thought his privileged position meant license to do whatever he wanted. He had believed another tragic lie.

Someone once said that freedom is like a coin. The word "privilege" is written on one side. On the other side is the word, "responsibility." There are too many today who want all the privileges, but refuse to accept any responsibility.

Amnon wanted the privilege of power without its responsibility. He wanted the excitement of sexual intimacy without the commitment of marriage. Rather than joy and freedom, he found destruction and death.

And the tragedy was set in motion because "Amnon had a friend."

Choose friends wisely

It's vital to choose friends carefully. Seek out Christian friends who will strengthen and encourage you. We all need a Barnabas or a Timothy to be there when we need him. This need for encouragement, in fact, is one of the principle motivators that should prod us to be a faithful part of a church:

> And let us consider how we may spur one another on toward love and good deeds. Let us not give up meeting together, as some are in the habit of doing, but let us encourage one another—and all the more as you see the Day approaching.
>
> Hebrews 10:24, 25

If you haven't got a Christian peer group—a home congregation and a small group within that local body—find one soon. Look for one that will support you, lift your spirits when they flag, and give you good advice when you need it.

Amnon had a distorted view of life. Self was at the center of his world, not God. What mattered most to him were his passions and his desires. He thought he was free and powerful. But he was pitiably weak. By saying "yes" to the evil advice of a supposed friend, he destroyed his own life and the lives of countless others. Scriptural warnings about evil friends are not to be taken lightly:

> Do not make friends with a hot-tempered man, do not associate with one easily angered, or you may learn his ways and get yourself ensnared.   Proverbs 22:24, 25

> A righteous man is cautious in friendship, but the way of the wicked leads them astray.   Proverbs 12:26

> He who walks with the wise grows wise, but a companion of fools suffers harm.   Proverbs 13:20

The scenario has been played out countless times through the centuries. The perils of peers can be devastating. Len Bias and Jim Bakker, I'm sure, would agree.

Be careful who you choose to be your friend. "Amnon had a friend"—and it cost him his life.

"The essence of immorality
is the tendency
to make an exception of one's self.**"**

Jane Addams
Social Worker and Nobel Laureate

"Temptations discover what we are.**"**

Thomas à Kempis

"Be self-controlled and alert.
Your enemy the devil
prowls around like a roaring lion
looking for someone to devour.
Resist him, standing firm in the faith,
because you know
that your brothers throughout the world
are undergoing
the same kind of sufferings.**"**

1 Peter 5:8, 9

Chapter Ten

The Lure of Lust

Lust is the ape that gibbers in our loins. Tame him as we will by day, he rages all the wilder in our dreams by night. Just when we think we're safe from him, he raises up his ugly head and smirks, and there's no river in the world flows cold and strong enough to strike him down. Almighty God, why dost thou deck men out with such a loathsome toy?

from *Godric* by Frederick Buechner[1]

We all struggle with temptation. We empathize with the little boy who was being punished by his mother for some misdeed. She took him by the shoulders, looked him in the eye, and said, "Honey, you've got to turn a deaf ear to temptation." With tears in his eyes, the boy protested, "But Mommy—I don't have a deaf ear."

None of us has a deaf ear.

No one is immune to temptation's seductive song. Like the sirens on the rocks that lured Ulysses and his men, temptations sing their plaintive melodies, beguiling our eyes and fogging our senses. Sometimes they parade before us in material ways, as money or the "finer things" in life. At other times, temptations are more personal and less visible, sneaking up beside us and whispering in our ear of power, prestige, or position. Others come wrapped in glamorous bodies appealing to our sensual natures. The apostle John summed them up well when he said:

> Love not the world, neither the things that are in the world.
> If any man love the world, the love of the Father is not in him.
> For all that is in the world, the lust of the flesh, and the lust of
> the eyes, and the pride of life, is not of the Father, but is of the
> world. And the world passeth away, and the lust thereof: but he
> that doeth the will of God abideth for ever.
>
> 1 John 2:15-17 *(King James Version)*

Temptations are part of the fallen world in which we live. They are as old as mankind. But in the past thirty years, a wave of sensuality has swept across our land. As Dr. James Dobson forcefully points out in his film, "The Family Under Fire," the pornography industry is reaping huge profits by dangling the lure of lust before our eyes. Like a fisherman's bait, it tempts us to bite. And once we're hooked, we're reeled in to destruction.

Blinded by lust's poison, kings have renounced their thrones, spouses their lifetime partners, and saints their God. Jim Bakker is just one of dozens of capable and respected ministers who have shipwrecked their faith on the rocks of immorality. And not long ago, in Southern California, two well-known Bible expositors and radio-personalities added their names to that ignoble lust.

A case study in lust

In the book of Judges, we meet a man whose life was destroyed by lust. A man of striking contrasts, we remember him today for two contradictory features—his physical strength and his moral weakness. His name was Samson.

In the days of the Judges, a new enemy, the Philistines, had just arrived from the island of Crete. This warlike people bequeathed the name "Palestine" as their lasting legacy to the land.

In their struggle with the Israelites, they seek a much more subtle domination than such earlier invaders as the Midianite camel raiders of Gideon's day. Through trade and intermarriage, they seek to bring the tribes in the southern part of the nation under their control.

God knows a deliverer is needed, and so He raises up a one-man army named Samson—a man who has a lot going for him.

1. He is blessed with godly parents.

Manoah and his wife are chosen by God to raise a special son because they are godly people. They do not question the message they receive from the angel, but simply set about discovering how best to comply with the angel's directions. They offer a burnt offering to the Lord and are overwhelmed with humility at the thought of being in His presence. After Samson is born, they stick to the strict Nazirite guidelines set for rearing him. Later, when Samson sets his sights on a Philistine girl, they attempt to point him to an Israelite bride as the Law commands (Judges 14:3).

2. He is set apart for the Lord from birth, specially consecrated to God's service:

> "No razor may be used on his head, because the boy is to be a Nazirite, set apart to God from birth, and he will begin the deliverance of Israel from the hands of the Philistines."
>
> Judges 1 3:5

According to Numbers 6:1-21, the Nazirite vow was a voluntary vow of devotion to God. The three requirements were:

(A) to abstain from all fruit of the vine

(B) to let your hair grow during the period of the vow and

(C) to avoid contact with dead bodies.

In this way, Samson is consecrated to God from birth. Ironically, he rarely keeps any of these vows—except for the one about not cutting his hair!

3. He is empowered by God:

> The woman gave birth to a boy and named him Samson. He grew and the Lord blessed him, and the Spirit of the Lord began

> to stir him while he was in Mahaneh Dan, between Zorah and
> Eshtaol.   Judges 13:24, 25

Since God has chosen Samson to be a judge and deliverer of Israel, He blesses him and equips him for the task.

Samson has an ideal preparation and beginning. But he also has a major character flaw he never is able to conquer—lust.

We first see him in action in the fourteenth chapter of Judges. He is a young man, probably around twenty years of age. Journeying down to the village of Timnah (about four miles from his home in Zorah, which was fourteen miles west of Jerusalem) he meets a Philistine girl and falls head over heels in "lust." Notice his first recorded words in Scripture:

> When he returned [from Timnah], he said to his father and
> mother, "I have seen a Philistine woman in Timnah; now get her
> for me as my wife."   Judges 14:2

From the start, Samson's nature had a bent toward sensuality. The attraction is entirely physical. He has never met her, only seen her. Yet he says to his parents, "Get her for me. She's the right one for me."

Samson is toying with lust, and that's a dangerous trap. It has such a grip on him, that he ignores God's Word forbidding intermarriage with non-Israelites (Deuteronomy 7:3, 4). Lust has him in such a vise, that he ignores his parents' pleadings that he marry a nice Hebrew girl (Judges 14:3). He has only one thing on his mind: "Gotta have that woman. Gotta have that woman."

His lust and sensuality are so out of control that they allow him to be a pawn in the hands of women. As a consequence, this first romance lurches toward disaster.

While traveling to Timnah, he kills a lion that attacks him. On a later journey he discovers that bees have transformed the lion's carcass into a beehive. It's filled with honey. This gives him a bright idea. At his marriage feast, he challenges his male guests with a riddle: "Out of the eater, something to eat; out of the strong, something sweet" (Judges 14:14).

The stakes are high—thirty outfits of "Sunday-best" clothes. But through threats and intimidation, his thirty "friends" force his fiancee to try to worm the riddle's answer from him. Using a combination of tears (seven days worth!) and that age-old line, "You don't love me!" she succeeds.

Off to a shaky start like that, it's no wonder the romance quickly disintegrates and turns tragic. Samson wreaks vengeance upon the Philistines. The escalating feud rocks back and forth until a large number of Philistines are dead, including Samson's former fiancee and her father (Judges 14:8—15:8).

Samson's immoral, sensuous, lustful lifestyle is filled with one problem after another. It's the nature of the beast. Sensuality doesn't lead to freedom, but to slavery. It can strike anyone at any time, but young adults like Samson are especially susceptible.

In addition to the young, there's another well-documented victim of lust—the man in a "mid-life crisis." We've already noted King David's problem with that particular crisis. And sure enough, the next time we meet Samson struggling with lust, he is middle-aged. It's twenty years later.

Apparently, he keeps his lustful appetite in check twenty years as he faithfully serves God and judges Israel (Judges 15:20). But then comes another round of passion's assaults—and Samson's mid-life crisis.

> One day Samson went to Gaza, where he saw a prostitute. He went in to spend the night with her. The people of Gaza were told, "Samson is here!" So they surrounded the place and lay in wait for him all night at the city gate. They made no move during the night, saying, "At dawn we'll kill him."
>
> But Samson lay there only until the middle of the night. Then he got up and took hold of the doors of the city gate, together with the two posts, and tore them loose, bar and all. He lifted them to his shoulders and carried them to the top of the hill that faces Hebron.
>
> Judges 16:1-3

Then it happens. After his escape from Gaza, he meets "her."

Someone once remarked that middle age is that perplexing time of life when we hear two voices calling us. One is saying, "Why not?" and the other is saying, "Why bother?"

Samson responds to the voice that says, "Why not?" and goes back to his old womanizing habits. He sets aside his morals and his God for a moment's pleasure.

This time he knows it's the real thing. Judges 16:4 tells us that "he fell in love," though "fell in lust" probably would be a more accurate description of the shallow, erotic love that binds Samson so tightly. The pretty thing's name is Delilah. You may have heard of her.

> The rulers of the philistines went to her and said, "See if you can lure him into showing you the secret of his great strength and how we can overpower him so we may tie him up and subdue him. Each one of us will give you eleven hundred shekels of silver."
>
> Judges 16:5

For a bribe that amounts, roughly, to something over five thousand dollars, Delilah agrees to ferret out the secret of Samson's strength so she might bind him and turn him over to the Philistine rulers. Notice that the English word used to describe her efforts in this verse is "lure." And she reels him in with consummate skill.

Three times she asks him for his secret, and three times he walks to the edge of the cliff, inching closer and closer to the edge each time (Judges 16:6-14). Samson is so blinded by lust that he fails to see the chasm into which he is about to fall.

Still, he manages to hold out. So Delilah finally pulls out the heavy artillery, "You don't love me!" (Judges 16:15). Now, where have we heard that line before? And so "with such nagging" she prods him day after day until he is "tired to death" (Judges 16:16). The old proverb once again proves true: "A continual dripping wears away the stone."

At last, Samson breaks down and tells all:

"No razor has ever been used on my head," he said, "because I have been a Nazarite set apart to God since birth. If my head were shaved, my strength would leave me, and I would become as weak as any other man."

When Delilah saw that he had told her everything, she sent word to the rulers of the Philistines. . . . Having put him to sleep on her lap, she called a man to shave off the seven braids of his hair, and so began to subdue him. And his strength left him.

Then she called, "Samson, the Philistines are upon you!"

Judges 16:17-20

He wakes up with a start, to battle the Philistines, "But he did not know the Lord had left him" (Judges 16:20). That has to be one of the saddest verses in Scripture. He thinks that nothing has changed. He believes he can toy with lust forever and never suffer any harm. He is so blinded by his passions and desires, he doesn't realize that the One who has blessed him and preserved him for so long is no longer with him.

And so the Philistines gouged out his eyes and set him to grinding grain. His lustful eyes will never wander again.

The fruit of lust

Lust is a destroyer. It binds you, blinds you, and grinds you till you're an empty shell of your former self. Samson's life, which began with so many advantages and in such promise, ends in helplessness and despair. The once mighty judge becomes a bald freak doing strong-man stunts at Philistine carnivals.

In our society, sensuality and lust are major problems. Sex is used to sell everything from cars to toothpaste. What is the annual best-selling issue of *Sports Illustrated?* The swimsuit edition, of course. The billion-dollar pornography industry also testifies to the strength of lust's lure. Slam the front door and it comes in the back. Turn off the TV, and it blasts through the radio.

Lust is no respecter of persons. No one is immune to its siren song. It attacks student and worker, single and married, the young and the old, the rich and the poor, pagan and Christian, all with equal impunity. I know two preachers who were best friends, until one had an affair with the other one's wife. As a result, two marriages and two ministries were annihilated. Chalk up more victims of lust.

Three observations

What can we do to combat this destroyer of hearts and minds? How can we withstand temptation? In the next chapter we'll learn some specifics from the life of Joseph. For now, here are three observations:

1. True freedom from sin is found only in Jesus.

When the apostle Paul wrote to the Christians in Rome, he said:

> What shall we say, then? Shall we go on sinning so that grace may increase? By no means! We died to sin; how can we live in it any longer? Or don't you know that all of us who were baptized into Christ Jesus were baptized into his death? We were therefore buried with him through baptism into death in order that, just as Christ was raised from the dead through the glory of the Father, we too may live a new life.
>
> . . .
>
> In the same way, count yourselves dead to sin but alive to God in Christ Jesus. Therefore do not let sin reign in your mortal body so that you obey its evil desires. Do not offer the parts of your body to sin, as instruments of wickedness, but rather offer yourselves to God, as those who have been brought from death to life; and offer the parts of your body to him as instruments of righteousness. For sin shall not be your master, because you are not under law, but under grace.   Romans 6:1-4, 11-14

If you are a Christian, you have a new master. Lust may offer temporary excitement, but Jesus offers permanent peace.

The quickest route to an unhappy life is to try to serve the Lord and our lust at the same time. Jesus said, "No one can serve two masters. Either he will hate the one and love the other, or he will be devoted to the one and despise the other" (Matthew 6:24). As Samson discovered, it just didn't work. His lust led to shame and humiliation, not to happiness and freedom. Choose Christ.

2. Remember who you are.

Lust is persistent. It kept coming back to Samson until it finally hauled him away. Make no mistake about it—lust will keep coming after you. So stay alert and remember who you are in Christ, and what He has and is creating in you:

> But just as he who called you is holy, so be holy in all you do; for it is written: "Be holy, because I am holy."
>
> 1 Peter 1:15, 16

The Bible urges us to be holy in our dating practices (1 Thessalonians 4:1-8), as well as in our marriages (Hebrews 13:4). Remember that you are a priest and a saint. Remember you have been "set apart," the basic meaning of both saint and holy, as special to the Lord. Samson forgot all that in the heat of passion and threw away his blessings and benefits.

Take God seriously and never forget who you are in Christ.

3. Remember that there is forgiveness with God.

It is never too late to repent and return to your heavenly Father. In the midst of mockery and derision, God heard and answered Samson's final prayer

> Then Samson prayed to the Lord, "O Sovereign Lord, remember me. O God, please strengthen me just once more, and let me with one blow get revenge on the Philistines for my two eyes."

> Then Samson reached toward the two central pillars on
> which the temple stood. Bracing himself against them, his right
> hand on the one and his left hand on the other, Samson said,
> "Let me die with the Philistines!" Then he pushed with all his
> might, and down came the temple on the rulers and all the peo-
> ple in it. Thus he killed many more when he died than while he
> lived.   Judges 16:28-30

Repentance can't always wipe out the harms and hurts of the
past; but it can build hope for the future. Never give up on
yourself. God doesn't.

A final warning

Although we remember him for his physical strength,
Samson's life is actually an example of weakness. Arthur
Cundall, in his commentary on Judges, sums it up well when
he writes:

> His life, which promised so much, was blighted and ulti-
> mately destroyed by his sensual passions and lack of separation
> to the Lord.[2]

Samson thought he could play with the fires of lust and not
get burned. He was tragically wrong.

Radio broadcaster Paul Harvey once described how an
Eskimo kills a wolf.

> First, the Eskimo coats his knife blade with animal blood and
> allows it to freeze. Then he adds another layer of blood, and
> another, until the blade is completely concealed by frozen blood.
> Next, the hunter fixes his knife in the ground with the blade
> up. When the wolf follows his sensitive nose to the source of the
> scent and discovers the bait, he licks it, tasting the fresh frozen
> blood, he begins to lick faster, more and more vigorously, lap-
> ping the blade until the keen edge is bare. Feverishly now,

harder and harder the wolf licks the blade in the night. So great becomes his craving for blood that the wolf does not notice the razor-sharp sting of the naked blade on his own tongue, nor does he recognize the instant at which his insatiable thirst is being satisfied by his own warm blood. His carnivorous appetite just craves more—until the dawn finds him dead in the snow![3]

Like that blood-soaked knife, lust kills. It entices us with a thirst that can't be satiated until it finally destroys us.

In the end, like Samson, we discover that lust is not a refreshing elixir. It's excitement is an illusion. We were only lapping up our own blood.

Chapter Eleven

When Temptation Knocks

A few years ago, a Gallup poll found that those disapproving of premarital sex had dropped from over two-thirds of the nation (68 percent to be exact) in 1969, to only 39 percent in 1985. One of the fastest growing demographic groups, as revealed in the 1990 census, are unmarried couples living together. And over the past twenty-five years, in spite of sex education in the public schools (some would say, because of sex education in the schools), venereal diseases and teenage pregnancies have skyrocketed. This last trend in particular has become a major concern in the mid-1990s, if an increase in media coverage and government rhetoric is any indication. What bothers me more than these trends in society is realizing that these same trends and attitudes are being displayed more and more openly in Christ's church.

As far back as 1984, George and William McKay documented a fact many of us had long suspected: that the values of our permissive society had, indeed, found a firm foothold among many apparently straight-laced church-goers. In their book, *Vital Signs,* based on surveys of those claiming to be "born again," Barna and McKay discovered that 23 percent of Christian households wired for cable television receive adult-only programming. In that regard, they observed, the Christian community is almost indistinguishable, percentage wise, from the non-Christian![1]

It appears that many Christians—not just young people—are fanning the flames of lust.

God created us as sexual beings. Sex is a wonderful gift and beautiful in the marriage setting for which God intended it. But, as Samson found out, it's something like fire. In a fireplace, it's warm and delightful. But out of the hearth, it's destructive and uncontrollable. Too late, Samson discovered that, as William Ward put it, "many of the world's most attractive temptations are like some television commercials: frequently deceptive and frightfully costly."[2]

Samson illustrates how not to handle sexual temptation. Now let's look at a young man who battled that temptation—and won!

A tale of temptation

Because Joseph was the favorite son of Jacob, his ten older brothers were consumed with jealousy, bitterness, and hatred. When they got the chance, they stripped him of his richly ornamented robe (his "coat of many colors"), tossed him into a pit, and would have killed him if it weren't for the pleading of the oldest brother, Reuben. Without shame or remorse, they switched to "Plan B," selling him as a slave to a group of merchants bound for Egypt. Then they dipped the fancy coat they so despised in goat's blood, and let their father think that Joseph had been killed by wild animals (Genesis 37).

Joseph entered Egypt as a piece of imported merchandise. There he was sold to Potiphar, "one of Pharaoh's officials, the captain of the guard" (Genesis 37:36). From Egyptian records, we discover that "captain of the guard" was an important post, which included overseeing criminal executions. Potiphar was definitely an Egyptian VIP!

But although Joseph's brothers have abandoned and forgotten him, and his future looks none too promising, One still stands by him: "The Lord was with Joseph and he prospered, and he lived in the house of his Egyptian master" (Genesis 39:2).

The story of Joseph in Egypt is one of those rags-to-riches, Horatio Alger stories. Undoubtedly, at first, he works at menial tasks. But as time goes on, he climbs the slave ladder of success and eventually reaches the top rung in Potiphar's household. Joseph appears to be the kind of worker described by the apostle Paul in Colossians 3:22-24:

> Slaves, obey your earthly masters in everything; and do it, not only when their eye is on you and to win their favor, but with sincerity of heart and reverence for the Lord. Whatever you do, work at it with all your heart, as working for the Lord, not for men, since you know that you will receive an inheritance from the Lord as a reward. It is the Lord Christ you are serving.

In trying circumstances, Joseph decides to make the best of it. He is motivated, cooperative, and intelligent, and God honors his faith and diligence.

As I've ministered in Southern California over the past twenty years, I've discovered that many employers, even non-Christian ones, recognize that dedicated Christians often make the best employees. I've received phone calls at the church office from employers, from gas station owners to department store managers, looking for honest workers. That's the kind of reputation believers should have, and that's the kind of employee-slave Joseph was.

That kind of worker eventually comes to the boss's attention, so Potiphar promotes Joseph until he reaches the position of personal aid, with oversight of the entire household (a position older Bible translations call a "steward").

Not only is Potiphar impressed with Joseph's work habits, he is impressed with his spiritual nature as well:

> When his master saw that the Lord was with him and that the Lord gave him success in everything he did, Joseph found favor in his eyes and became his attendant. Potiphar put him in charge of his household, and he entrusted to his care everything he owned.   Genesis 39:3, 4

How does Potiphar "see" that the Lord is with Joseph? Has he seen him regularly kneeling in prayer, as some will later observe of Daniel (Daniel 6:10)? Has he been closely watching Joseph's attitudes and behavior, observing that they are far above those of his other slaves? Is it Joseph's spirit of honesty and truthfulness? Whatever the cause, Potiphar knows that there is a spiritual dimension to this young man that contributes to his character and work habits. He makes Joseph, in effect, his "executive assistant," and his household is richly blessed (Genesis 39:5, 6).

Unfortunately for Joseph, Potiphar isn't the only one who notices him:

> Now Joseph was well-built and handsome, and after a while his master's wife took notice of Joseph and said, "Come to bed with me!"   Genesis 39:6, 7

Not only is the Hebrew kid a sharp businessman, he is also quite a "hunk." (Lust can attack women too, can't it?)

What is the problem with Potiphar's wife? Why is she so smitten by this young slave? Perhaps she's reacting to that all-too-common problem of the absent husband: "Potiphar is always gone on the Pharaoh's business. He has no time for me. He doesn't love me. He isn't meeting my needs." Scripture doesn't reveal the cause of her wandering eye. Whatever her excuse, she succumbs to temptation.

Temptation is not sin. Jesus was tempted as we are, yet never sinned (Hebrews 4:15). Yielding to temptation is what's sinful. As Chuck Swindol puts it, "It's not the bait, it's the bite."

James outlines temptation's pattern:

> Each one is tempted when, by his own evil desire, he is dragged away and enticed. Then, after desire has conceived, it gives birth to sin; and sin, when it is full-grown, gives birth to death.   James 1:14, 15

Whatever her rationalizations, Potiphar's wife believes in the direct approach. Succumbing to temptation, she demands, "Come to bed with me!" But Joseph resists:

> "With me in charge," he told her, "my master does not concern himself with anything in the house; everything he owns he has entrusted to my care. No one is greater in this house than I am. My master has withheld nothing from me except you, because you are his wife. How then could I do such a wicked thing and sin against God?"   Genesis 39: 8, 9

Joseph's refusal is impressive for several reasons:

1. He is young and single, living in a pagan environment.

Even his upbringing and home life had its share of immorality. It would have been easy to rationalize and "go with the flow." But he doesn't.

2. Potiphar's wife is persistent.

Genesis 39:10 tells us, "Though she spoke to Joseph day after day, he refused to go to bed with her or even be with her." This sort of daily dripping is what Delilah used to wear down Samson's resistance. Yet Joseph refuses to yield.

3. Joseph doesn't have the spiritual insight you and I have— or even what King David had, for that matter.

Joseph lives more than four hundred years before God gives the Ten Commandments. He has no Bible at all. He is, in fact, busy living out a portion of what will become the first book of God's Word. But he clings to the light he has: God's basic morality implanted in his being, and the teaching of Abraham, Isaac, and Jacob.

Joseph gives Potiphar's wife two reasons for refusing her advances. One was human, the other divine. First, he refuses to violate Potiphar's trust (vv. 8, 9). Second, he can't disobey God (v. 9). He knows the double dimension of this evil and he refuses to yield to it.

Actually, the two reasons are interrelated. Potiphar knows of Joseph's faith and convictions (v. 3). To violate Potiphar's trust would be a terrible witness and would undoubtedly undermine any faith that might be growing in his heart.

Joseph's reasons for refusing to yield have been some people's rationalizations for yielding. Freedom from supervision can be a good cover for sin. Others (such as Eve) have regarded the areas barred to them (whether by God or society) as objects of frustration, not of honor. "After all," they say, "rules were made to be broken."

But Joseph is not that kind of person. He refuses to yield to her temptation.

The chance for the "perfect set-up" finally arrives. Potiphar's wife stops asking and pleading and takes action:

> One day he went into the house to attend to his duties, and none of the household servants was inside. She caught him by his cloak and said, "Come to bed with me!" But he left his cloak in her hand and ran out of the house.   Genesis 39:11, 12

Joseph doesn't waste time talking. There is no way that he can politely refuse, so he leaves his cloak instead of his skin and gets out of there on the double!

Some in the religious world teach that if a person follows God, everything will be fine and dandy. God will bless you with health and wealth, they say. But Scripture doesn't make that claim, at least not about what might happen in this world. Joseph's next experience reminds us that obeying God can lead to trouble and persecution.

Joseph gets "framed" (Genesis 39:13-20). The old proverb, "Hell hath no fury like a woman scorned," is well illustrated by Potiphar's wife. She has been turned down by a Hebrew slave—slave, mind you—and she is outraged! In her fury, she turns on him and cries, "attempted rape!"

To resist temptation and receive a pat on the back is one thing. But to resist temptation and receive a slap in the face is quite another. When Potiphar hears his wife's story, he is furious. He throws Joseph into the special prison reserved for the king's prisoners.

Potiphar could have Joseph executed, but he doesn't. Why not? Perhaps he has some misgivings about his wife's charges. A woman as persistent as she is most likely has had "difficulties" before. Still, Potiphar has to save face, so Joseph is dragged off to prison.

Yet, even in prison, the Lord is with him (Genesis 39:21). Once again, Joseph starts rebuilding his life, working his way up yet another ladder of success.

Many types of temptation

Although Joseph's temptation was primarily sexual, other factors were involved. He was also tempted in regard to power and position. To resist Potiphar's wife could (and did) cost him his job.

The times when we are most successful, whether financially, socially, vocationally, or even spiritually, are often the times when we're most vulnerable to temptation. When things appear to be at their best, the worst in us, or around us, may trip us up. That was the situation with David and Bathsheba, and it could have been the cause of Joseph's downfall.

God had granted Joseph success, but that blessing did not insulate him from Satan's attack. Scripture warns, "Be self-controlled and alert. Your enemy the devil prowls around like a roaring lion looking for someone to devour. Resist him, standing firm in the faith" (1 Peter 5:8, 9).

When things are going well, it's easy to get cocky and let down our guard. Pride rises in our hearts, and we can become an easy mark for Satan's fiery darts. Paul warns us, "So, if you think you are standing firm, be careful that you don't fall!" (1 Corinthians 10:12). Because temptations are a constant part of life, and Satan is our never-resting enemy, we need to be alert and on guard constantly.

When temptation knocks

What practical lessons can we learn, then, from Joseph to help us fight temptation?

1. Be aware

> Finally, be strong in the Lord and in his mighty power. Put on the full armor of God so that you can take your stand against the devil's schemes. For our struggle is not against flesh and blood, but against the rulers, against the authorities, against the powers of this dark world and against the spiritual forces of evil in the heavenly realms.   Ephesians 6:10-12

We must realize that Ephesians 6 is not a bit of first-century superstition, but an accurate portrait of reality. We are engaged in spiritual warfare, and our enemy wants to draw us from God and watch us fall.

Ultimately, Satan is the one behind temptations. That's why Scripture calls him "the tempter" (1 Thessalonians 3:5). Therefore, we are commanded to resist the devil and his temptations, not to tolerate them: "Submit yourselves, then, to God. Resist the devil, and he will flee from you" (James 4:7)

We need to be aware of the reality of spiritual warfare. It's nearly impossible to win a battle when you don't realize you're in a war. When temptations strike, too many Christians are caught as off guard as the United States was at Pearl Harbor, December 7, 1941. Be aware!

2. Be prepared

Once we're aware of the reality of spiritual warfare and the fact that no one is immune, we need to prepare for the fray. How?

It's essential to develop a close, working, and walking relationship with our Commander-in-Chief, the Lord Jesus Christ. Immediately after James exhorts us to resist the devil, he writes:

> Come near to God and he will come near to you. Wash your
> hands, you sinners, and purify your hearts, you double-minded.
> Grieve, mourn and wail. Change your laughter to mourning and
> your joy to gloom. Humble yourselves before the Lord, and he
> will lift you up.   James 4:8-10

Draw close to the Lord in humility.
We also need to be dressed for the spiritual battle before us:

> Therefore put on the full armor of God, so that when the day
> of evil comes, you may be able to stand your ground, and after
> you have done everything, to stand. Stand firm then, with the
> belt of truth buckled around your waist, with the breastplate of
> righteousness in place, and with your feet fitted with the readi-
> ness that comes from the gospel of peace. In addition to all this,
> take up the shield of faith, with which you can extinguish all the
> flaming arrows of the evil one. Take the helmet of salvation and
> the sword of the Spirit, which is the word of God. And pray in
> the Spirit on all occasions.   Ephesians 6:13-18

The closer we are to God and the better we know His Word,
the more likely we are to be sensitive to the convicting ministry
of the Holy Spirit when we are confronted with temptation. It
then will be easier to discover God's solution to our problems
and frustrations, rather than Satan's tempting shortcuts.

I have a friend who is a marriage, family, and child counselor.
He once shared with me his observation that, among Christians
he counseled, the farther they drifted from a daily relationship
with God, the more trouble they had in dealing with problems.
Then he said, "People don't bring problems into counseling.
The problem is their solution. The farther they stray from seeking answers in God's Word, the worse their solutions and the
worse their situation."

From the biblical record, Joseph appears to be a believer who
maintains a close walk with God, no matter what trials and
temptations come his way. Because of that relationship, he

knows what he believes even as the attempted seduction begins. He is determined not to violate Potiphar's trust in him, nor to sin against the Lord. Here is a reminder to each of us: there are people about us—family, friends, co-workers, Christians, and non-Christians—who count on us not to yield to temptation. We are responsible to them, as well as to God. Because of God's love and grace, we must say "no" to temptation:

> For the grace of God that brings salvation has appeared to all men. It teaches us to say "No" to ungodliness and worldly passions, and to live self-controlled, upright and godly lives in this present age.   Titus 2:11, 12

3. See and flee!

Mark Twain once quipped, "There are several good protections against temptation, but the surest is cowardice." Funny, yet there is a godly truth to it. Fear can be a God-given warning light, for many things in this life worth fearing. The consequences of sin are certainly among them (Proverbs 14:12; Romans 6:23). Joseph had the good sense to run from temptation. Perhaps Twain would have called it cowardice. I prefer to call it a realistic acknowledgment of the power of sin. Certainly God's Word encourages us to see and flee!

> *Flee from sexual immorality.* All other sins a man commits are outside his body, but he who sins sexually sins against his own body. Do you not know that your body is a temple of the Holy Spirit, who is in you whom you have received from God? You are not your own; you were bought at a price. Therefore honor God with your body.   1 Corinthians 6:18-20

> Therefore, my dear friends, *flee from idolatry.*
>   1 Corinthians 10:14

> *Flee the evil desires of youth,* and pursue righteousness, faith,
> love and peace along with those who call on the Lord out of a
> pure heart.   2 Timothy 2:22

But we must flee more than the obvious enticements of Satan—*flee fantasy* as well. We must avoid verbal and visual stimuli in our battles against temptation. Learn from Joseph who "refused to go to bed with her or *even be with her*" (Genesis 39:10).

While we can't avoid temptation, we have some controls over our surroundings. This is one reason I found the statistics from *Vital Signs* so disturbing. Far too many Christians are inviting lust and sensuality into their homes, hearts, and minds. This is the area where Samson blew it. He allowed himself to be under temptation's constant attack until he finally yielded to the pressure (Judges 14:7; 16:16). What makes us think we are any stronger than he was?

In *Clergy Couples in Crisis,* David Seamands writes, "Every case of unfaithfulness starts . . . in rationalizing that fantasy is allowable. . . . Fantasy is like a beachhead from which the rest of the island is attacked."[3] Archibald Hart of Fuller Seminary's School of Psychology adds, ". . . sexual fantasy, in my opinion, is dangerous because it leads to obsessional thinking. . . . Fantasy is the beginning of perversion."[4]

Temptations, in and of themselves, are not sin. But we have a choice regarding our response to them. Will we resist and flee? Or will we encourage them by fantasizing, by playing with them in our hearts and minds?

Scripture commands us to keep our thought lives clean and holy, "Above all else, guard your heart, for it is the wellspring of life" (Proverbs 4:23).

> Finally, brothers, whatever is true, whatever is noble, what-
> ever is right, whatever is pure, whatever is lovely, whatever is
> admirable—if anything is excellent or praiseworthy—think
> about such things.   Philippians 4:8

Let's quit playing with fire. If certain films, music, or magazines arouse your passions, avoid them. If certain places, events, or friends lead you into sin, avoid them. Get rid of "adult" cable channels. In other words, if you're on a diet, don't go into doughnut shops!

Don't tolerate in your life what can eventually destroy it.

A closing thought

God will not forget those who resist temptation. Rely on Him. He wants to help:

> No temptation has seized you except what is common to man. And God is faithful; he will not let you be tempted beyond what you can bear. But when you are tempted, he will also provide a way out so that you can stand up under it.
>
> 1 Corinthians 10:13

> Submit yourselves, then, to God. Resist the devil, and he will flee from you.   James 4:7

When facing temptation, we can find hope and strength in the Lord. People won't always understand when we resist. Some may criticize, saying we're "old-fashioned." Others may ridicule, calling us "puritanical." But God will honor our faith. He did Joseph's. The young "hunk" eventually became the number-two man in Egypt.

Let's imitate Joseph, not Samson. When temptation knocks, flee.

And don't leave a forwarding address!

"Blessed is the child of yesterday.**"**

Ronnie Milsap and Mike Reid
"Old Folks"

"Hope I die before I get old.**"**

Peter Townsend and The Who
"My Generation"

"Gray hair is a crown of splendor;
it is attained by a righteous life.**"**

Proverbs 16:31

Chapter Twelve

Silver Threads Among the Gold

In July of 1985, Leslie Hypes of Anaheim, California, sat down with a cassette recorder and made, in part, the following tape:

> This is Leslie W. Hypes. . . . Elsie and I were married forty-five years ago and we had two different ceremonies to make it absolute legal. At both ceremonies we made our vows until death do us part, in sickness and in health, for better or for worse. . . . Three years ago, Elsie went totally blind and since then she has been a very unhappy person. And two years ago, she started having visions, possibly caused from hardening of the arteries, although at the time it was thought that it was an over-dose of prednisone. . . . But recently it has come back on her worse than ever and she has been so unhappy. There are little images of men, animals, that keep fighting her all the time. And she is in constant agony. She does not get to sleep at night and she has begged me many times to give her some sleeping pills so that she can end it all. She wants to die. She prays every night to die.

Elsie was eighty-seven. Leslie had just turned eighty-eight. Blindness had brought bitterness to Elsie's life. Instead of "golden years," she and her husband had found a cold, inhospitable world. Shortly before 6:00 P.M. on July fifteenth, Leslie Hypes called a friend and said, "Stan, come right over, I need you." The friend found both of them dead from gunshot wounds. A .38 caliber revolver lay in Leslie's lap.[1]

When this story appeared in 1985, 11.8 percent of the United States population was sixty-five or older. Yet that age group accounted for 25 percent of the nation's suicides.[2] Unfortunately, the situation hasn't improved in the last decade. When Kurt Cobain, leader of the rock group, Nirvana, killed himself in 1994, *Newsweek* magazine did a cover story on the subject of suicide. Although the article focused on Cobain and other young adults, a comparison of teen deaths to those of the elderly was revealing:

> The figures [for suicide have] remained stable in this country since the end of World War II. . . . The rate for teenagers, after climbing steeply for two decades, began leveling off in the mid-1970s. . . . The only groups going against the grain are black males and the elderly, especially white men over sixty-five. . . . *The suicide rate for the elderly is higher all over the world than it is for teenagers and young adults* (emphasis mine).[3]

Clearly, for many, the "golden years" are days of helplessness and hopelessness. Loneliness, depression, isolation, pain, and fear mark the lives of many elderly people, pushing them toward the possibility of suicide. Since the publication of the Hemlock Society's, *Final Exit,* in 1991, the use of this "suicide cookbook" has become an open secret in the retirement communities of Southern California.[4]

We are all subject to aging. Growing older is an indisputable fact of life. But it's a reality we can handle in many different ways. Robert Browning, for instance, put the following words into the mouth of his poetic character, Rabbi Ben Ezra:

> Grow old along with me!
> The best is yet to be,
>   The last of life, for which the first was made:

> Our times are in His hand
> Who saith "A whole I planned,
>> Youth shows but half; trust God:
>> see all, nor be afraid!"

Is there a Christian response to the process of aging? Are there any guidelines in Scripture that can help?

According to God's Word, growing old should not be something we despise or fear. Rather, for the godly, aging should be an honorable thing. Proverbs 16:31 says, "Gray hair is a crown of splendor; it is attained by a righteous life." In Proverbs 20:29 we read, "The glory of young men is their strength, gray hair the splendor of the old."

In my personal experience, it was easier to read those verses before my hair started graying than since the silver threads appeared among the "gold"! Why? Because I am as subject to the pressure of our contemporary American culture as you are, and the message of our society is, "Comb away the gray," and "Get rid of the wrinkles." The message that constantly bombards us is, "It's great to be young, and terrible to be old."

Myths about aging have so inundated us that Dr. Michael Halbertstan, an expert in the field of geriatrics, has said, "Fear of growing old may well be the worst affliction of advancing age."[4] Our attitudes and expectations about growing older make the major difference in how we handle it. The English preacher/writer, Jonathan Swift, captured the essence of the dilemma when he said, "Everyone desires to live long, but no one would be old."

Demographics reveal that not only are we all growing older as individuals, but America is graying as a nation as well. Since 1900, medicine and technology have extended the average American's life span by twenty-six years. These population changes can be pictured as follows, with birth and childhood at the bottom of each figure progressing upward through teens and adults to the most elderly at the top.

In the 1800s, when the life span was shorter, the population looked like a pyramid with lots of children and youth, but a relatively small number of adults.

 In the 1950s, the population began to swell up like a barrel with growing numbers of young and middle-aged adults.

 By the end of this decade and the start of the new millennium, the population will look like a light bulb with large numbers of older adults.

The biggest change and challenge will come as the baby boomers age and start retiring in the year 2011. It is estimated that, come A.D. 2020, 20 percent of the nation will be over the age of sixty-five.

All of us—young as well as old—should decide now how we will cope with the aging process. Will it be with fear and thoughts of suicide? Or will it be with faith and courage that, indeed, the best is yet to be?

What is old?

Old, of course, is a relative term. Just what is old? One of the prevalent myths about aging is that one is automatically "old" at age sixty-five.

The truth is that the chronological measurement of age is the least important measurement. Psychological, intellectual, and physiological aging are much more significant.

I was watching a Super Bowl game a couple of years back when a player was singled out because the game would be his last. He was retiring—at the ripe old age of thirty-seven! And I thought to myself, "Hey! Hold on a minute. I'm thirty-seven!" That may be old age in professional sports, but ages thirty-five to fifty-five are considered prime years in business, ministry, and most other professions.

No one is automatically "old" at sixty-five. There are still tremendous possibilities for growth and creativity. Some studies out of U. C. Berkeley and other schools across the nation indicate that senility is definitely not inevitable. The Berkeley studies reveal that some brain experts are beginning to adopt a "use it or lose it" philosophy. Ongoing research shows that continued mental challenges can lead to larger brains, healthier cells, and more efficient thinking.[5]

The researchers are saying that we're never too old to learn! Keep an open mind and an inquisitive spirit. "Use it or lose it"!

Plenty of examples—both contemporary and biblical—prove that old age doesn't have to be a time of inflexibility and deterioration:

✔ Colonel Sanders was in his sixties when he began expanding his Kentucky Fried Chicken business and sold his first franchise.

✔ Jack Benny's agent dropped him when he turned seventy-one. He thought Jack was all washed up. Benny found a new agent and completed twelve million dollars in bookings before he died at the age of eighty-one.

✔ Verdi composed his opera *Falstaff* at the age of eighty.

✔ Moses was eighty when God called him to lead the children of Israel out of Egypt. Aaron was eighty-three when he became Israel's first high priest.

✔ Will Durant completed the last volume of his *Story of Civilization* at the ripe young age of ninety.

✔ Arthur Rubinstein was still giving piano concerts into his nineties (as was Eubie Blake, the jazz pianist).

✔ Picasso was still painting at ninety-one.

✔ Grandma Moses was still painting at 101.

✔ And, to return to the field of sports, the world was electrified in November, 1994, when George Foreman (at the ripe old age of forty-five) became the oldest heavyweight champion ever, knocking out Michael Moorer, a man half his age. As one editorial commented, "He set a new standard for the supposed limits of life." Or, as another headline expressed it, "He's paunchy, he's slow and he's forty-five—and that's just fine."

The list could go on and on.

A study out of the University of Wisconsin has said that if a person stays physically well and keeps active, he can get as much out of life at ninety as at forty. That points to an important key to aging "gracefully"—the realization that the preparation for aging is a lifelong process. While many of us prepare financially for retirement, how many prepare mentally, physically, and spiritually?

In the Old Testament, we meet a fascinating person who was prepared.

When we first meet Caleb, he is one of the twelve spies sent into Canaan by Moses (Numbers 13). After checking out the possibilities of an Israelite conquest, only two of the twelve believed God would give them the victory: Joshua and Caleb. Look at Caleb's faith:

> Then Caleb silenced the people before Moses and said, "We should go up and take possession of the land, for we can certainly do it."   Numbers 13:30

At the time, Caleb is forty years old—moving into middle age. But because of his faith, God promises Caleb that he will enter the land of Canaan and gain an inheritance in that place of milk and honey (Deuteronomy 1:36).

Forty-five years later, after the wilderness wanderings and five years of campaigning under Joshua to conquer the land, it is time to divide it. While Joshua is hard at work, parceling out the land allotments to the various tribes, Caleb comes up to him with a very special, and most unusual, request:

> "Now then, just as the Lord promised, he has kept me alive for forty-five years since the time he said this to Moses, while Israel moved about in the desert. So here I am today, eighty-five years old! I am still as strong today as the day Moses sent me out; I'm just as vigorous to go out to battle now as I was then.

> Now give me this hill country that the Lord promised me that
> day. You yourself heard then that the Anakites were there and
> their cities were large and fortified, but, the Lord helping me, I
> will drive them out just as he said."   Joshua 14:10-14

"Give me the tough area with the giants," (which is what the Anakites were). What a man of faith—and at the age of eighty-five! He had lived a life of faith in the past, and now he is ready to do what he said all along could be done. He's ready to defeat these giants that made his ten fellow spies quake in their boots and feel like grasshoppers.

Caleb isn't just a lot of talk. He had said, forty-five years earlier, "We can do it." Now he is ready to fulfill that prediction:

> From Hebron Caleb drove out the three Anakites—Sheshai,
> Ahiman and Talmai—descendants of Anak. From there he
> marched against the people living in Debir (formerly called
> Kiriath Sepher). And Caleb said, "I will give my daughter Acsah
> in marriage to the man who attacks and captures Kiriath
> Sepher." Othniel son of Kenaz, Caleb's brother, took it; so Caleb
> gave his daughter Acsah to him in marriage.   Joshua 15:14-17

He does get a little help from his future son-in-law, but that just helps to speed up his war. As someone quipped, "The old can do anything the young can do—it just takes longer."

Before someone tries to excuse himself by saying, "Yeah, but that was back when people naturally lived longer!" let me point something out. According to Moses, the average life span in his day had come down from the pre-flood life spans to the exact same range as our day. A few individuals, such as Moses, did live past one hundred years, but the days of real longevity were gone with the flood. In the only psalm he wrote, Moses put it this way, "The length of our days is seventy years—or eighty, if we have the strength" (Psalm 90:10)—so no excuses or rationalizations out there!

As young as your faith

You are as young as your faith, hope, and self-confidence. . .
or as old as your doubts, fears, and despair. Douglas MacArthur
said this well on the occasion of his seventy-fifth birthday:

> In the central place of every heart there is a recording cham-
> ber; so long as it receives messages of beauty, hope, cheer, and
> courage, so long are you young. When the wires are down and
> your heart is covered with the snows of pessimism and the ice of
> cynicism, then and only then have you grown old.[6]

The choice is yours and mine. Don't get a "retirement" mind-
set that makes you think you are no longer able or needed in
the Lord's service. I've met too many Christians (and not always
older ones) who have the attitude, "I did my bit. Let someone
else take over now; let someone else teach, visit . . . ." You finish
the sentence and fill in the blank. That attitude is sad, and it's
also unbiblical. If you are still breathing, Christ still needs you
serving in His army.

Fortunately, I've known many others who have found that
aging opens new doors of opportunity for service to Jesus
Christ. I know some in their seventies who are now actually
busier in Christ's kingdom than ever before!

✔ I remember meeting Pearl Williams in the late 1960s
when I was a student at Pepperdine University's original cam-
pus in south central Los Angeles. Pearl had been born in
Jefferson County, Alabama, in 1869. A diminutive black
woman, she began working with the Spastic Children's
Foundation in Los Angeles when she was in her eighties. There
she taught the children crafts and handiwork. A member of the
Compton Avenue Church of Christ, she decided she "wanted to
be alive and do something for other people." So, in 1972, at the
age of 103, she joined the Foster Grandparent Program. She was
honored for her work with that group on her 106th birthday by
then first lady Betty Ford.

✔ I know of a group of retired Christians who travel

throughout the United States in their campers, visiting small, struggling congregations and helping out in as many ways as they can. They call themselves, "The Sojourners."

✔ When I ministered with the Sunny Hills Church of Christ in Fullerton, California, many of the retired members taught Bible correspondence courses to people living around the globe. Two, who were retired schoolteachers, had over five thousand students between them. Every year there were dozens of conversions because of their efforts.

✔ And I remember Ralph Treas. Ralph was the bookkeeper at that same church. He was retired from his secular job, but not from the Lord's work. He took a small salary as a supplement to his Social Security, but his real work was in short-term missions. Not only did he have a number of Bible correspondence students, but once a year he would go with a group to Ghana in West Africa and spend four to six weeks following up on his (and many other) eager students, teaching, sharing and personally leading many to salvation in Christ. In the time we worked together, he made four trips—his first at age seventy-two!

What makes the difference?

Why do some end their lives in bitterness, loneliness, and sometimes suicide? And why do others—the Calebs and Pearls and Ralphs—keep going strong to the end, conquering new lands for God?

Psychologist Erik Erickson has said that late adulthood is a time for introspection: it's the time when we decide between what he called integrity and despair. It's the time when we reflect on our lives. If life is viewed as good, with positive accomplishments, we move into the last years with hope. But if life is viewed as disappointing, with few accomplishments, we move into our last years with despair.

The foundation of faith, hope, and trust in God is laid in our early years. Caleb knew that. So did Douglas MacArthur, who said:

> People grow old only by deserting their ideals. Years may
> wrinkle the skin, but to give up interest wrinkles the soul.
> Worry, self doubt, self distrust, fear and despair; these are the
> long, long years that bow the head and turn the growing spirit
> back to dust.

Whatever your age, be thankful for it. Sow spiritual seed as well as financial for the future. Plan to stay spiritually young, whatever your chronological age. Keep your mind active and your hands useful.

Ever since I was "forced" to read it as a freshman in college, one of my favorite poems has been "Ulysses." In it, Alfred Lord Tennyson pictures the Greek hero feeling famous, but useless as an idle king living out his sunset years. He's ready for new adventures. He's ready to start growing again! Speaking to his sailors, he says:

> . . . You and I are old;
> Old age hath yet his honour and his toil;
> Death closes all; but something ere the end,
> Some work of noble note, may yet be done,
> Not unbecoming men that strove with Gods.
>
> . . . .
>
> . . . Come, my friends,
> 'Tis not too late to seek a newer world.
> Push off, and sitting well in order smite
> The sounding furrows; for my purpose holds
> To sail beyond the sunset, and the baths
> Of all the western stars, until I die.
> It may be that the gulfs will wash us down;
> It may be we shall touch the Happy Isles,
> And see the great Achilles, whom we knew.
> Tho' much is taken, much abides; and tho'
> We are not now that strength which in old days
> Moved earth and heaven; that which we are, we are;

> One equal temper of heroic hearts,
> Made weak by time and fate, but strong in will
> To strive, to seek, to find, and not to yield.

There are still great victories to be won for Christ. There are still good works to be rendered to others. The golden years can be the crowning of a life of faith, integrity, and courage. Like Caleb and Ulysses, don't yield. Keep striving, keep seeking, keep discovering. And never give up.

"Carry on, my wayward son, there'll be peace when you are done.**"**

Kansas
"Carry On My Wayward Son"

"Therefore, since we are surrounded by such a great cloud of witnesses, let us throw off everything that hinders and the sin that so easily entangles, and let us run with perseverance the race marked out for us. Let us fix our eyes on Jesus. . . . Consider him who endured such opposition from sinful men, so that you will not grow weary and lose heart.**"**

Hebrews 12:1-3

Epilogue

American Airlines Flight 199 glided peacefully over the Arizona desert. Some passengers sat eating what remained of their meal. Others, having just finished, yawned and stretched. All anticipated landing in San Diego, California, within the hour—with loved ones to greet or business deals to complete.

Suddenly, a tremendous "bang" ripped the afternoon air. The Boeing 727 shuddered violently. The passengers sat in frozen terror. One, John M. Smith, later expressed what must have been going through all their minds: "I thought I was dead . . . I thought, 'What a terrible last meal.'"

After what seemed an eternity, the pilot spoke over the intercom. An engine, he said, had "stopped turning." Not to worry. They were descending from thirty-five thousand to twenty-six thousand feet and they would still make it safely to San Diego.

What the flight crew didn't realize was that an engine had done more than stop turning. One of their three-thousand-pound, tail-mounted power plants had ripped loose and fallen off somewhere near Gila Bend, Arizona. Not until the jet taxied up to the ramp at Lindbergh Field did the ground crew discover an engine was missing.

That story is a good metaphor for life. Things go wrong. Depression engulfs us with terrifying swiftness. Fear creeps into our hearts with chilling effect. Friends let us down. We thought we'd be forever young (didn't we even sing a rock song with those words?), but the body slows down as the years fly by. Plans go awry. "Engines" fall off. Sometimes we find ourselves knee deep in one of life's cesspools, fighting enraged gophers.

But don't overlook this fact: Flight 199 did make its destination! As the story hit the evening news, Boeing revealed that, when necessary, its 727 is designed to fly on the power of just two engines. If one engine seizes, its bolts break off, allowing the engine to fall rather than twist and rip the plane's frame to pieces.

Our Maker designed us better than a Boeing 727. He created us to keep flying despite the storms and stresses of life. We can carry on. Some rest, proper maintenance, and occasional repairs undoubtedly are needed for the journey, keeping in mind that we never should attempt to fly too long on just two engines. But the human spirit is tough and resilient. Our God constructed us in such a way that we, by His strength and wisdom, can find the courage to carry on.

I hope this book has encouraged you. I hope you've found in it some words and ideas to help repair damaged engines. I hope you've found some practical principles and actions you can apply as you climb out of a cesspool. I hope it has given you courage to hang in there one more day, to seek God's guidance one more time, to trust Him more, even when the crazed gophers attack, even when your life shudders and you think, "We're all gonna die!"

Hang in there. Don't quit.

I like Smith's attitude. He was still eating lunch when Flight 199 went bang: "I thought 'What a terrible last meal.' I figured I had three minutes to live, so I ought to enjoy it. I finished my chocolate brownie and milk."[1]

Carry on. Find courage in the Lord to fight life's battle.

NOTES

Introduction

1. "A Night in Deep Trouble." *South Bay Daily Breeze* (22 Jan. 1985): A3.

Chapter 1

1. John F. Kennedy. *Profiles in Courage*. Memorial Edition. New York: Harper and Row, 1964.

2. Cerise Valenzuela. "Scout's Honored." *Orange County Register* (26 Dec.—27 Dec. 1990): News 1, 5.

3. Charles Swindol. *Growing Strong in the Seasons of Life*. Portland: Multnomah Press, 1983.

4. Kennedy, 266.

Chapter 2

1. Doug Bandow. "War of the Worlds." *Orange County Register* (30 Oct. 1988): J1.

Chapter 3

1. O. Hobart Mowrer. *The Crisis in Psychiatry and Religion*. Princeton: D. Van Nostrand Company, Inc., 1961.

2. Archibald Hart. *Feeling Free*. Old Tappan: Fleming Revell Co., 1979.

3. C. S. Lewis. *Mere Christianity,* first paperback edition. New York: Macmillan Publishing Co., 1960.

4. Hart, 143.

5. Paul J. Jordan. *A Man's Man Called by God*. Wheaton: Victor Books, 1980.

Chapter 4

1. J. Leo. "Sudden Death." *Time* (30 July 1984): 90-91.

2. Annie Nakao. "Mass Murderers: They're Angry, Bitter, Desperate." *Orange County Resister* (29 Jan. 1989): A3.

3. S. I. McMillen. *None Of These Diseases*. Old Tappan: Fleming H. Revell Co., 1963.

4. Ibid., 67-68.

5. Earl Ubell. "The Deadly Emotions." *Parade Magazine* (11 Feb. 1990): p. 5.

6. McMillen, 72.

7. H. Norman Wright. *Communication: Key To Your Marriage*. Ventura: Regal Books, 1974.

Chapter 5

1. Greg Zoroya. "A 'Perfect' Family's Life Turns Tragic." *South Bay Daily Breeze* (23 Dec. 1984): A1, A3.

2. Don Baker and Emery Nester. *Depression: Finding Hope and Meaning in Life's Darkest Shadow*. Portland: Multnomah Press, 1983.

3. Clyde Narramore. *How to Handle Feelings of Depression*. Grand Rapids: Zondervan Publishing House, 1969.

4. Baker and Nester, 35.

5. Sidney Jourard. *The Transparent Self,* 2nd ed. New York: D. Van Nostrand Company, 1971.

Chapter 6

1. Mike Gordon. "A Fateful Shot." *Orange County Register* (4 Feb. 1993): E1, 2.

2. Redford and Virginia Williams. *Anger Kills.* New York: Time Books, 1993.

3. Ibid., 3-14.

4. Batsell Barrett Baxter. *Anchors in Troubled Waters,* 32. Grand Rapids: Baker Book House, 1981.

5. Jeffrey Miller. "Ty Cobb—Hit Man With an Attitude." *Orange County Resister* (15 Oct. 1994): Show 3.

Chapter 7

1. James Dobson. *Hide And Seek.* Old Tappan: Fleming H. Revell Co., 1974.

2. William Glasser. *Reality Therapy.* New York: Harper and Row Publishers, 1965.

3. Archibald Hart. *Feeling Free.* Old Tappan: Fleming H. Revell Co., 1979.

4. Steve Bisheff. "Olson Will Go to Any Heights," The *Orange County Register* (16 Jan. 1986): D1.

Chapter 8

1. Alan Loy McGinnis. *The Friendship Factor,.* Minneapolis:

Augsburg Publishing House, 1979. Used by permission of
Augsburg Fortress.

2. Susan Aschoff. "Men Believe Intimacy a Sign of
Weakness." *South Bay Daily Breeze.* (5 June 1985), quoting
Michael McGill, author of *The McGill Report on Male Intimacy:*
C2.

3. Cartoon by Doug Hall. *Leadership,* (Winter 1985): 54.

4. Aschoff, "Men believe intimacy," C2

5. C. S. Lewis. *The Four Loves*. New York: Harcourt, Brace and
Company, 1960.

6. Quoted by Paul Robbins. "Must Men Be Friendless?"
Leadership, (Fall 1984) 28.

7. Lewis, *The Four Loves,* 103.

8. McGinnis, *The Friendship Factor,* 9.

9. Frederick Buechner. *Peculiar Treasures: A Biblical Who's
Who*. San Francisco: Harper and Row, 1979.

Chapter 9

1. Nancy Cooper, Bob Cohn, Mark Starr and Shawn Doherty.
"The Mystery of a Star's Death." *Newsweek* (30 June 1986): 29.

2. Lloyd Cory. *Quotable Quotations*. Wheaton: Victor Books,
1985.

3. Charles Shepard. Forgiven: *The Rise and Fall of Jim Bakker
and the PTL Ministry.* New York: The Atlantic Monthly Press,
1989.

Chapter 10

1. Frederick Buechner. *Godric*. New York: Atheneum, 1980.

2. Arthur E. Cundall and Leon Morris. *Judges, & Ruth: An Introduction & Commentary,* 181. Downer's Grove: Inter-Varsity Press, 1968.

3. Submitted by Christ T. Zwingelberg. "To Illustrate." *Leadership,* (Winter 1987): 41.

Chapter 11

1. George Barna and William McKay. *Vital Signs*. Westchester: Crossway Books, 1984.

2. Lloyd Cory. *Quotable Quotations,* 393.

3. Dean Merrill. *Clergy Couples in Crisis*. Waco: Word Books, 1985.

4. [Forum discussion with] Arch Hart, Louis McBurney, Bud Palmberg, and David Seamands. "Leadership Forum: Private Sins of Public Ministry," *Leadership,* (Winter 1988): 23.

Chapter 12

1. Martin J. Smith. "Undying Love, Mortal Anguish in Anaheim." *Orange County Register* (9 Dec. 1985): B1.

2. Ibid.

3. David Gelman. "The Mystery of Suicide." *Newsweek,* (18 April 1994): 48

4. Tracy Weber. "Taking Control of Death as They Did Their Lives." *Orange County Register,* (14 Feb. 1993): A1.

5. Quoted by M. Norvel Young in "Don't You Believe It!: Myths About Aging." *20th Century Christian* (Nov. 1978): 5.

6. Allen S. Keller. "Doctors Adopting 'Use It or Lose It' Philosophy Toward Brains." *Orange County Register* (7 Jan. 1987): E1, E8.

7. Cory. *Quotable Quotations,* 19.

Epilogue
1. Author. "Passengers Describe Terror as Engine Tears Loose from Jet." *South Bay Daily Breeze* (17 April 1985) A9.